Wanting in Arabic

poems

Trish Salah

Introduction by Lisa Robertson

We acknowledge the support of the Canada Council for the Arts for our publishing program. We also acknowledge support from the Government of Ontario through the Ontario Arts Council.

We acknowledge the financial support of the Government of Canada through the Canada Book Fund for our publishing activities.

  Canada

Cover design by Christa Seeley

Library and Archives Canada Cataloguing in Publication

Salah, Trish, author
        Wanting in Arabic : poems / Trish Salah ; introduction by Lisa Robertson.—Second edition.

ISBN 978-1-927494-30-1 (pbk.)

        I. Title.

PS8587.A319W36 2013   C811'.6   C2013-904888-X

Printed and bound in Canada by Coach House Printing

TSAR Publications
P. O. Box 6996, Station A
Toronto, Ontario M5W 1X7
Canada
www.tsarbooks.com

Contents

Enduring This Future

Trish Salah and the Andalusian Uncanny

In a culture that is fenced by capital, by imperative identifications, by the violent sexualization of bodies, by the institutionalization of resistance, and perhaps most intensely by a generally proscribed historical amnesia, how can we love what is absent in language, absent in politics? What is lyric's terrain? I'd like to claim for lyric poetry the anachronistic space that Ammiel Alcalay opens for Hebrew culture: "It seems to me that the only chance for Hebrew culture is to grow backwards: to bring to bear all the power and richness it can muster from the past by losing the fear of reaching the point of freedom it takes to be traditional." But what does Alcalay mean here by "tradition"? We are accustomed to the weighting of the term with the most orthodox and conservative values, but here Alcalay's tradition refers to the exploded foundations of the heretical cultural heterodoxy called al-Andalus: Al-Andalus, the eight-century-long intensively intercultural peace on the Iberian peninsula, the south of France, and Sicily, the culture that ended in 1492, with the beginning of the Spanish inquisition and the torture, forced conversion and assimilation, or expulsion, of Jews and Moslems from their ancient European home.

It's a mostly overlooked fact that there was a strongly Arab Europe, beginning in the eighth century. This culture's violent suppression has now continued for six centuries, arguably in a continuum with the current series of American and Israeli wars. But al-Andalus, a passionately discursive heterodox utopia that did exist, that can exist in the free movement of forms of language, continues. What could it mean for poetry to grow backwards towards it?

Palestinian poet Mahmoud Darwish said, "Andalus might be here, or there, or anywhere," and Adonis, the Syrian Poet, said "Andalusia seems a viable project, not only for the present, but also for the future." Juan Goytisola is a creator of al-Andalus in what he calls "the fertile territory of doubt;" Alcalay is also, with his claim for the freedom of tradition; the Hebrew scholar and translator Peter Cole is, the French linguist Henri Meschonnic was, in his life of thinking through a prosody of geopoetics. The anarchic passion of Stacy Doris was Andalusian, pointedly so, when she spoke of the necessity of delusional space. And Trish Salah's poems are part of the work of al-Andalus. These are lyric poems that speak with great risk, across cultures. They posit a subject that accrues a life in movement, in open exchange. In this reading of Trish Salah, I hope to show that the work of lyric is Andalusian.

Lyric has undergone a willful misrecognition within avant-garde poetry-reading and critical communities. I can't subscribe to the now-typical reactive train of thinking that places lyric in negative, abject, and ideologically naive relation to a positively conceived aesthetic of affirmative experimentation, conceptualism, or innovation. Binary, hierarchical, and reductive systems of thinking in this way can't be part of a liberatory poetics. Nor am I interested in recuperating lyric via a dialectic procedure, where a "new" third position arises from the fluctuation between and synthesis of oppositional practices. Emphatically too, lyric does not promote or bolster or found any singularity of voice: rather it disperses, exchanges, de-centres, mimes, and multiplies voice, and by extension subjectivity, which I will define here as the sited, bodily, and recursive aptitude of an historical speaking among and towards others. I read Trish Salah's work as lyric, meaning: an exiled voice speaks towards its condition, invents a contingent authority that dissolves into receiver after receiver, mimics centres in order to disperse them in a lucid pleasure, slows down its legibility because it wants to install useless and indeed anti-utilitarian agencies of perverse instability in its readers. I'm using the word perverse in Roland Barthes' sense: the search for a pleasure that is not made profitable by a social end or benefit. The organs of the lyricist will always be outside the polity. Rather than defining essences, seeking an originating aesthetic ontology of lyric (the dubious and reactionary misadventure of a Heideggarian reading of poetics), I would like to shift the discourse around lyric from the field of aesthetics, weighted as it is, in the contemporary poetry world, with invisible, unstated ideologies, positions, and in-fights, to the field of culture, in order to see how lyric moves culturally, how it has moved historically, remembering also that history is what issues from that mobile, shapeshifting and pleasurable organ, the mouth. History is what speaks. In fact, we could consider lyric as a dialect, in the sense that there is only dialect, and no language. Speech is a continuous movement, alteration, of constellations of human specificity. Language is only the dialect that is politically privileged and accordingly fixed, removed from the vocal and historical continuum and framed by an institutional matrix. For the time being, let's consider lyric as a dialect. Lyric the dialect evades the fixity of language. It does this in part through a principled mis-use of form. Pertaining not to the stability and authority of a fixed grammar, and not necessarily to the often iterated materiality of language, lyric form coheres as rhythm coheres—only in movement, within a contingent and multi-valent temporality, like a pattern that gradually transforms its own composition as it moves towards other patterns, by substitution, various kinds of rhyme, citation, partial appropriation, intensification, and counterpoint. Perhaps the cogency of lyric is its immateriality. Voice can move under cover, "in the guise of." Formal or rhythmic tendencies lend a temporary situatedness, or a potential exchangeability, to the unbounded affect of a voice that fully responds to a containment, an ejection, a mis-identification. This voice seizes tradition as an improvisatory present. Ironically the return of lyric to culture restores to the poem the flourishing and contestatory agencies of desire. In the poem desire can re-radicalize the aesthetic, bring it back to the threatened tradition of the body. A lyric culture will always be wildly embodied.

From her home wander love's uncanny away, you!
Is it past: whose to tear memory away, you?

The oppressive weight of reactionary tradition derives not from the energy of tradition's forms (form is always energetic), but from the orthodoxy, and sometimes violence, of the enforcement of particular versions of historical cultures and grammars, particular writings of history, versions that usually serve to authorize and support the tyrannies of nation, identity, church, and patriarchy, those most unsecular ideologies. Goytisola's description of a contemporary al-Andalus as the mobile terrain of "fertile doubt" points to the radically immaterial agency that burns through the ideological posturings of a spuriously applied pseudo-tradition as a court of judgment, a rigor mortis of the mind. In fertile doubt we arrive afresh at the ancient site of a multiplicitous, heretical, and oppositional secularism that lifts and lives through and in the movement of rhythmic or formal motifs. This is the lyric of al-Andalus. We can grow backwards towards it.

To be clear: Al-Andalus needs no territory, occupies no geography. It is a wandering continuity of voices speaking among other voices. Even its pronoun works a wandering:

From her home wander love's uncanny away, you!
Is it past: whose to tear memory away, you?

Trish Salah shows us al-Andalus as the exploded foundations of the body, the body with a heart in it, the body pulsing with juice and desire and temporality. Shall we call it Hydromel? Cyprine, in Nicole Brossard's coinage? A Vernacular? The vernacular, Dante tells us in *De vulgari eloquentia,* is the language we learn at the breast, the language learned from women and spoken by children, without the aid of rules and grammars. It was the dialect whose nobility he argued for and wrote within, in a seemingly radical reversal of the canonical superiority of Latin. It is also the dialect whose beauty he discovered retroactively, while in exile from Tuscany and mother tongue. In *De vulgari eloquentia,* written during his exile (1302), he makes the still-provocative claim that Latin is a synthesized, imposed, and even ficto- grammar, not a foundational language, and that the Romance vernaculars did not descend from this authorized and most ancient set of language rules and codes, but accompanied it; there was always a variability of spoken Romance dialect traditions existing in tandem with the written Latin grammar, a wandering continuum of soft codes carrying along the political fiction of an authorizing grammar. For Dante it is the moving, vernacular tradition that precedes and over-flows hard grammatical code. Radically, he privileged the popular. His argument for the vernacular found its precedent in the lyrics of the Provençal poets, poets who themselves were on the outer edge of the rich hybridity of al-Andalus. In describing the presence of the Proven-çal lyricists in his thinking, he said they were like honey to his water; the sweet love of the vernacular was hydromel, he said, a drink both refreshing and intoxicating. Several decades later, beginning in 1327, Petrarch too wrote in a Romance vernacular, in the south of France, before he repudiated his cycle of youthful songs to Laura to return to composing in the authoritative Latin. He was writing near the time of the first printing presses in Italy; Aldus, the Venetian printer, and the originator of small-format pocket-books for a general reading public, turned Petrarch's vernacular songs into a contemporary popular best seller, consciously supplying a vernacular linguistic focus for a gather-ing Italian national identity. This wresting of national languages from the fluid variability of spoken vernaculars is often seen as the begin-ning of a certain modernity, the end of medieval confusion; this is how the Italian vernacular writers were placed within a certain dominant narrative of European literary traditions. But from the perspective of al-Andalus, this appropriation of the lyric vernacular in the fifteenth Century into national identity formation represented not a beginning but an ending, or at best a contradictive solidifying of what had been an extremely long and mobile counter-tradition.

The medievalist scholar Maria Rosa Menocal constructs a narrative for this deeply suppressed tradition, the tradition in which vernacular song, circulating in an ancient context of tricultural hybridity, across myriad dialects as well as the official grammars, and in a region of intensely speculative intellectual discussion, pedagogy, translation, institutional organization, and publication in the areas of philosophy, science, mathematics, psychology, and medicine, becomes the lyric poem. This is the lyric poem our avant-gardist cultures are often quick to repudiate.

From her home wander love's uncanny away, you!
Is it past: whose to tear memory away, you?

One of the parenthetical discussions in Menocal's *Shards Of Love: Exile and the Origins of the Lyric* concerns the medieval conception of time, history, and memory. She describes this as a temporality of simultaneousness, where the past *lives* co-determinant within the present, and where memory activates its traces, so that the sense of the present and the future are composed and made vital by memory. In such a temporality, the past is not an unfortunate limitation to be rendered distant, detached, by progress and the fetishized production of newness. Rather, "the past is constituted by immediate and powerful memory traces that make sense of the present and the future." That these traces constitute the vitality of form is at the core of my arguement, but before going deeper, I'd like to at least indicate the political fact and effect of the severance of the present from the past, the severance enacted repeatedly by a cult of newness and innovation. That the place of Arab and Hebrew cultural forms and life are unacknowledged or politically stigmatized within European historiography constitutes such a historical severance. To what extent is the ubiquity of innovation as a Western cultural and social value an iteration of the exilic severance enacted in 1492? Lyric memory is cultural memory.

From her home wander love's uncanny away, you!
Is it past: whose to tear memory away, you?

The popular song-form of early medieval al-Andalus was called the *muwashshahat*. These multi-lingual songs enacted lovers' dialogues, using rhyme, a device never before used in Arabic, Hebrew, or Latin. Each song included a *kharja,* or refrain, composed in a vernacular that until recently was not recognized as such, but was assumed to be a nonsensical and musical gibberish, not a semantic contribution to the verbal meaning of the poem. This *kharja* has now been recognized, according to Menocal, as a transcription of the oral dialect spoken commonly by women, Mozarabic. So the *muwashshahat* is a diglossic, high/low, bastard, and doubly sexed song form, and is now hypothesized to be the mother of Troubadour and Provençal lyric song, with its rhyming motifs, conversational structure, and presentation of the love dynamic as an oral exchange between sexes, not a singular voice to be represented in a unified language. In contrast to the extremely rich translation culture surrounding medieval Arabic and Hebrew philosophical, scientific, and other high-culture textual forms, *muwashshahat* were not translated; there is little material evidence to prove the routes of transmission from the Iberian peninsula, across the Pyrenees mountains through the Languedoc region, the centre of the great heretical counter-tradition of the Albigensians and Cathars, and from there, into Provençe. But the *muwashshahat* were popularly sung in the common speech, so their formal traits were mobile, adaptive, and, Menocal posits, foundational to the vernacular lyric tradition of late medieval southern Europe, the tradition that invented that other traveling form, the sonnet, and became the Western lyric poem as it has been transmitted through these few centuries to our contemporary moment.

It seems important to me at this point to emphasize the strongly gendered transmission tradition of the lyric form. The vernacular refrain sung by Andalusian women, or sometimes by men singing as women, that led to Dante ennobling the language of women as the lyric language, was part of a very long tradition of women's song in the Mediterranean regions. In research I did many years ago on the origins of extended simile in the Homeric epic, I learned about the origin of simile in Bedouin women's mourning songs. In these songs, simple couplets, or *bayts*, repeated with slight patterns of organic variation, compared the beloved, lost to death or war, to various animals. Some Homeric scholars speculate that Bedouin women's *bayt* was the source for Homeric simile. The word *bayt* means song couplet, and it also means tent, a nomadic tent woven by women of goat hair. The *bayt*, divided inside by a decorative woven partition into men's and women's parts, made of the temporality of loss, and of nomadism, a temporarily bordered space that was also a couplet. The language of weaving and poetry, their shared rhyme and metrical repeat, their shapeliness, detailed surface quality, and continuity, was the daily vernacular of women, not the language of grammatical authority, and as such, travelled, was adaptable, moved into and across other traditions.

In making this side excursion to a sketch of a gendered Arabic and Bedouin song tradition, I don't intend to posit some fundamental claim in the lines of an essentialism. Rather I want to point to a specific cultural history of form, in order to be better able to notice its wandering, its capacity to shape-shift. Another name for this shifting continuity of form is subjectivity.

From her home wander love's uncanny away, you!
Is it past: whose to tear memory away, you?

The subjectivity that moves through the lyric poem, the pronominal twisting, is what moves language across identities to disperse them, to continuously transform any posited stability in favour of a heretical speaking *through, among,* and *into.* Who speaks? Who receives? Song speaks and receives. The subject sings only towards another subject, and in this way there is a person. The French linguist Émile Benveniste's theory of subjectivity in language makes an excellent reversal, parallel in a certain way to Dante's reversal in value of the authorized and vernacular tongues. Benveniste says that speech is prior to subjectivity, not vice versa, and that the effect of subjectivity is a property of language, not an ontological a priori:

The "subjectivity" we are discussing here is the capacity of the speaker to posit himself as "subject." [. . .] Now we hold that that "subjectivity," whether it is placed in phenomenology or in psychology, as one may wish, is only the emergence in the being of a fundamental property of language. "Ego" is he who says "ego." That is where we see the foundation of "subjectivity," which is determined by the linguistic status of "person." (SiL, 224)

For Benveniste, subjectivity is not anchored in the individual; subjectivity is an attribute of language. As such, there is no opposition between the individual and the social:

And so the old antinomies of "I" and "the other," of the individual and society, fail. It is a duality which it is illegitimate and erroneous to reduce to a single primordial term, whether this unique term is to be the "I," which must be established in the individual's own consciousness in order to become accessible to that of the fellow human being, or whether it be, on the contrary, society, which as a totality would preexist the individual and from which the individual could only be disengaged gradually, in proportion to his acquisition of self-consciousness. It is in a dialectic reality that will incorporate the two terms and define them by mutual relationship that the linguistic basis of subjectivity is discovered. (SiL,225)

Benveniste's theory of the mutuality of the speaking subject arose from a set of basic differentiations he insisted upon, differentiations between meaning as signification, and meaning as open exchange, and by extension, the basic differentiation between semiotics and semantics, or discourse. For Benveniste, language was not only a system of signs, not a fixed set of arbitrary binary equivalencies between signifier and signified, in Saussure's terms, but a movement of meaning by a subject who was himself constituted by the meaning she transmitted. Yet he did not privilege the linguistic capacity, but considered that language is a human trait, always has been a human trait, inseparable from the complex history of corporality and the life of the senses. This enlivened and volatile concept of linguistic subjectivity becomes even more stimulating to apprehend if considered formally. The shapes of language emit or cite us as subjects as we transmit those shapes in time. We in this way arrive at an anachronic practice of lyric temporality similar to the medieval one, where memory traces activate a past and a future simultaneous to the present. And we arrive at a formal tradition of the lyric as a charged multivalent temporality of the bodily subject, lyric as a heretical secularism, lyric as powerful weapon against universalizing grammaticism, lyric against the fixing of identity, against the reign of a grammar of unity. We can call this unity Europe, America, the Market, the enforced coding of sexuality as a closed binary system. We can call it whatever we like—any such grammar of unity imposes its inquisition upon the mobility of a desiring body, a politically and historically specific body that inhabits a formal movement in order to be charged with a flourishing variousness. Through lyric the body is enduringly heretical. This is the free tradition I attribute to Trish Salah. It is the uncanny tradition of al-Andalus.

From her home wander love's uncanny away, you!
Is it past: whose to tear memory away, you?

Lisa Robertson,
Berkeley-Toronto-La Malgache
(note: an earlier version this text was
presented at the invitation of Margaret
Christakos in her Influency salon, in 2009)

Works Cited

Alcalay, Ammiel. *Memories of Our Future: Selected Essays 1982-1999.* Introduction by Juan Goytisolo. San Francisco: City Lights Books, 1999.

Benveniste, Emile. "Subjectivity in Language" in *Problems in General Linguistics.* Trans. Mary Elizabeth Meek. Coral Gables; University of Mi ami Press, 1971. Originally published in *Journal de psychologie 55* (July September 1958).

Dante Alighieri. *De vulgari eloquentia: Dante's Book of Exile.* Mariane Shapiro. Lincoln and London: University of Nebraska Press, 1990.

Menocal, Maria Rosa. *Shards of Love: Exile and the Origins of Lyric.* Du ham, NC & London: Duke University Press, 1994.

Salah, Trish. *Wanting in Arabic: Poems.* Toronto: TSAR Publications, 2002.

Wanting in Arabic

Phoenicia ≠ Lebanon

Phoenicia ≠ Lebanon
though they occupy the same place, more or less
    a) on a map? *do you see*
      b) in my heart? *to the west, the accident*
        c) in this poem, Phoenicia ≠ Lebanon? *that holds you down?*

    i have never been to Lebanon *before i was*
though i have often dreamed of Phoenicia *dreaming in this world*
the cedar groves, the long low galleys *my father was*
bazaars raucous with a thousand tongues *born in Lebanon (≠ Phoenicia)*
& before Lebanon was
Babylon by any other—all too Greek for me.
& though he did not die
there, in Phoenicia, or, in Lebanon
i am my father's daughter *(few return from that voyage*
May he rest in— *like Odysseus, from the sack of—*
to die, comforted in his own bed)

who, as a small boy, intimidated at the prospect of the priesthood—
of following in my father's footsteps
until they ceased to be his—
he only made it to the seminary,
before he came across the Atlantic transformed *May he rest in—*
in the middle passage, like the Phoenicians, perhaps
in their long low—
never to return—not without my mother & she,
before him
Irish Catholic, with her own "troubles"
you can't get there from—

perhaps that's the origin of my infatuation with high heels
or better, mary janes,
eschewing the Jesuits' cassock
for convent girl plaid

what i never could figure,
my brothers had it worse & they didn't turn out
sissy boys, she-hes, homo
sexuals, or, as in my case,
lipstick lesbians.
were they not raised for dodging bullets, racist dogma,
the Christian Phalange, to fight for ruined
Beirut against all odds, against Muslim, Palestinian?
after Daddy's death, precocious, they studied the way of the warrior,
or its suburban equivalent, Tae Kwon Do,
the Tae Kwon Do twins used their powers
to protect their too femme older bro'
strutting the corridors of St Pat's High,
neither a phobic bone, nor a homo
between their strapping young bodies.

so maybe it wasn't my father's plans for us
that got me so queer
maybe it was a child's premonition
of his stroke at 37
an immigrant's death of stress, a high salt diet, a foreign tongue
and, let's face it,
too many years of eighteen hour days
or perhaps it was smaller
just the way his mouth got tight about
his voice strangled and raging at
a 5 year old's inability to sleep
i'm not unsympathetic, who wouldn't
be frustrated by chronic insomnia in a child so young?
anyway, who cares why
i ended up my daddy's little girl?

i ended up my daddy's little girl   *didn't i?*
heartbreaking, he didn't live to see the day & the boy
i was, caught dead in a crossfire in Beirut or Belfast
prostrate before my pretty Mohammed   *ever after*

4

and nothing to do with Phoenicia
or Lebanon, but ex-girlfriends'   *and after my surgery comes*
memories of a childhood, Cypress   *that boy's dead by any other name*
where my cousins also fled   *you know what the dead do best is rise*
                                                    Phoenix-like, again

a June War in '67
and, called
to return to Lebanon
where i have never been
my name should be *Phoenicia*
i'll prefer Yismine, for my aunt's sake.
for shame's sake, my French, my Arabic will mime strangers' tongues

missing my father's tongue.
the Phoenicians were the ranging traders of another world
on the news tonight shelling in this Lebanon,
    a trampled marketplace
                    a strategic site
occupied by the French, the Americans, the Syrians, the Israelis
and Beirut is a hole in the ground through which the past comes up

                                        (nevertheless,
                                my cousin Nada says,
        never you mind, cuz, some of the richest people in the world
                in that city. it will be beautiful and whole again,
                                        give it five years
                                just you wait and see!)

i stole this poem from Robert Kroetsch
but don't feel sad about it, he wasn't
Phoenician & even at sea, even trading
in words, in the past, in love, in the middle passage
                                        in the in between
i'm not either
but am i Lebanese?
not like that dyke comic,
do you remember her? playing coy,

Ellen? the TV lesbian?
who, coming out on Rosie O'Donnell
was either Lebanese or lesbian, on TV or off
(lesbian≠Lebanese≠TV)
except, perhaps, as in my case
where, sure, say it:
i am
a) Lebanese
b) lesbian
c) TV
d) all of the above
e) none of the above

so much for that

Wanting in Arabic

I

Face down in the deep olive   crush
to my tongue   yr imagined melting

What I can want is just to learn
just what learning is, though

With Dr. Freud, express a little pessimism
at our prospects.   Before the band, tell jokes.

At hand, suddenly your touch, surprised, wrest
from my wrist, surprised, and you were?

So you don't know? I don't.   I,
was thinking of Beirut—   *of returning.*

II

When they were kids, they said, sharing
trauma, the unveiling memory can be

Oh you? you too?   Touch to the hurt again,
what is possible for them again, here.   Sisters.

On the drive back, you quarreled, styles
of loving. Good thing I wasn't along.

My old confidante knows the flush
longing gives my voice, the eager cadence

and how I turn bitch in a fight that matters.
Suppose, annoyed, we looked away, burst into Arabic?

III

What then? you might ask, wordless or or
cautious like the glass blower wanting it made perfect

the so slow sortie, the measure of your gaze   held
perhaps in repetition in duration   enduring

our first kiss will be a definition,
te'berini. I cannot say it, but a life

Becoming   made of breath. Delirious
thought as a symptom, your object,   mine.

And breathless from speaking, *habibte*
and me foolish, silent before our common languish.

IV

Presents you might give me:
a grammar and salt, your tongue, tumbling

not crashing, recipes for mint and cinnamon
lamb skin at thighs, kindling memory

scripting, scrolling, fearless hands, be longing
meaning's double, resilient regard, your dance.

Presents I might give you:
blood urgent with hunger, measured

be longing, the comfort and cut
of teeth, these two bodies (male, female),

graciousness with other lovers, fresh bread,
argument hot with Arak, stories, resilient regard.

V

Oh linger here, warming my breath, secreted
furtive moment of fingers, clasped, released

for the day. It's enough, today, strangely to grow
like this, desire's plunge and deepening moment

You and I twined in looking, tender intake
roaring quiet under our friends' clever banter.

Shadows warm more than December sun
shadows blanket us. Until we might peel one,

another, press to heat winter skins, trembling
beneath glances like hands, hands.

VI

That day you crossed the field on your way to
stand over me. She and I did not

admit the division that you, unwitting,
carried instead of groceries. I didn't say

will you come, to her apartment, to any   where
shadows grow deeper   gather us in.

After you, I made my own excuses. Startled, tasted
how relentless and zealous this wanting could be—

I made my way home, hoping for a chance—
A second.

VII

How to read my remoteness in November
but regard for your lover, your integrity?

(I know now you were not reading
with me, not with eyes open, but

it's a poem, okay? Memory has an interest
and eros and the unconscious, so, anyway—)

and, yes, fear was there too, and, perhaps
uncommon sense. The same reason, dear one

I (won't) love your woman for what she
is to you.   *Do you guess I do?*

VIII

Sometimes a girl forgets her own self,
what to make of her own body.

You remind me—
with your body's recognition of its own, my own

near or far, psyche's other place, either direction
or, if you like, home,

will do. It doesn't matter; a body knows
when it should be elsewhere; why not?

A girl can get stretched thin, not knowing how
to get there— *there*. Where you are

IX

We have our secrets, or they have—
as passion circles, surrounds. We don't

put it out, call it gone, swallow large as we make
off.   It will not yield.

Passion knows we breathe, what to do.
Goes airy and unseen the better to enter

you and I, our verging inward
maps, folding old futures, in. Might we

be eaten and eat, my dear? As pomegranates
quicken awhile longer, come, inside me, you.

X

So   beloved. Do you want? *Objects:*
I write "i want you,"

and you know there is no more desolate thing.
How to say what it takes to give us a long time?

Enough to learn, to kiss your half open lips   open
where and how you're soft, what's hard,

to let fingers run the ridge of your collar bone
eyes been angling along while and fall, fresh

nuzzle night into dawn down   where
you're cunt & belly & legs, we are beginning

XI

Just so you know, I'm a bad genealogist,
always taking effects for causes   *for desire:*

Triangles are the last thing, the first
figures I may learn from you as my own

or you may, near me, falling in my arms,
out of root, *en route*   equations' relay

(triangulations, duplicities, the singularity
of want of you) if not family,

the semblance, loosening trees   roots   splitting?
desire can't help but wander, remainder itself

XII

Of course I don't speak Arabic. It is
no guarantee, however I mine genetic memory

along a chill sweat skein, and heart sprung loose and
pounding yes I know   you   may not   even now

risk that desire, not be poised to call to
answer to—   It is a vast leap.

I do believe it.   Oh, but your caress—
What's at risk? Is risk

your spine? Mine? What is brought spinning un—
seen, mere shimmers there, between us?

                              Not peace, i think

Ghazals in Fugue

I

From her home wander love's uncanny away, you!
Is it past: whose to tear memory away, you?

Stolen upon thought, "I'll not see the end of this."
Ya aa'yni, turn your gaze from me away, you.

A girl's hand may stop unexpected, bleeding over
What, wrest, was—eye to eye, between, a way, you . . .

Fall mistaking what looks she tosses for salvation.
Beware such boasts, what they give too freely away, you.

Unhinge the doors, with talk of children, your double, war;
Send memory's limbs flailing. Who cast peace away, you?

II

Hear the sound of rain, on hotel window, so stark it bleeds
Like waking, like Hitchcock? Blinds so low, it's too dark to read.

Here, the train breaking haunts, further out, the frame, broke hours ago.
What are Effrit to make twin towers glow, too dark to read?

Disfigured, losing specific dimensions, failing
In their finitude, what world is mirrored, too dark to read?

As fire works, roaming compulsive, the mind makes interior,
What was your house, her tomb, charred terribly, too dark to read.

There your girl becomes pursuit, embers, a route more circuitous
Her elliptical and fraying parabola. Too dark to read

Such hyperbole of desire. Fire returns void, in its avoidance.
Brute motor repetition writes parables too dark to read.

III

Into the wilds, some cliché of the wilds . . . it's not the war
We flee, north, from Toronto—that year we're not at war.

Gone to cottage like white folks, and compose queer idylls, break
Our fast at the Colonial, stock up at Nassr; say that's not war.

With our weight in lebne, mint, parsley, burgle, beans for ful, lamb
For kibeh, we beg no guarantee of country. Anything but war

Until the third bottle of wine, allows someone to ask
If, in Lebanon I am that man, if not, that war,

My father wanted. You want to know what bargains
With snow will I make? Were my cousins not in that war?

Would I not have been with them, at Sabra, at Shatilla?
Naïve to the war, I break all our glasses, this ghazal's form, smiling.

IV

In the commons we give up on speaking, fall quiet
Cast looks to the mountains; from the pool, all's quiet.

More to hold us here, than memory, or will, allow.
Lying by, in glassed-off heat, we listen past fall's quiet

Whispers' crackle, a jammed radios' abandon, as mute,
Iraq's young succumb to deserts "we" let fall . . . Quiet

As, when we slump into the sauna, genitals swaddled
White cotton shrouds, all eyes avert. Quietly appalled,

Afraid to see my breasts, yours, to site black dick. In the north
Country, we feel what they fear, the weight of whiteness, falling.

(quiet)

V

Beyond the compound, illegible to itself, the war
Asks its children to hold it. Who holds still to read a war?

Caught in our race each day, we have our watchers. Behind blinds,
Driving by, attentive as dogs or cops, they ask, like in a war,

At the movies, if we are spies, "What do they want? Why are they here?"
We ask the same questions. They're different questions prised from war.

We listened to Miles in the car, awed by mountains at war with . . .
Years, miles away, as if New York wants for terror, this Afghan war.

Slaughter all fanatics, the misogynists, and history too;
They're no longer in our pay, there's no balm—our grief like war.

Whitman praised your sensuous and muscular form, but the body
Which moves because the mind cannot, fugues the world as war.

To answer your question, they are the same: America, war.
A different war, to hold it at bay, even this question of war.

Without signs of home, what is our common destination?
The commonplace of departure? Do we tarry out of love with war?

VI

The letter left on the kitchen table, signed your love,
"This is an invitation." You both knew what it was. Your love,

How could she follow? There was no place. If sharing a war,
Our parents' flight, night train whispers, all were glamour, love

Where I stand not so far from you, like one merely looking on
I wonder what else you may need let fall. Glower, love

I'm just cautious, knowing soon I may warrant these ruins:
How may a city become bereft? Is that evening the score, love?

Your misery begs the question. She could have come, you lament,
She had an invitation. So slim sheaves make out of paper, love.

Mistaking the world's history for your own, you still think
Something was said, somewhere. About you. About her. Poor love.

VII

In fugue or bastard ghazal, she is seeking no place like home.
When language becomes a girl, she speaks for a voice like home.

As we were, sweet with wine, spiraling need, commanded from home
You plaited, out of sight, a sex; below stars swam light down, home.

A nervous girl, no less in love than in her mother's own home.
In finely stretched olive skin, she becomes less, and less at home.

Foreign names your distrust: old sorrows drawn out, poise to steal home.
Finger a war fetish; drink deep, slake—of her red Real—your "home."

Where do you go when she speaks? Your story recoiled from home—
Less errant than in orbit yoked—wanes, jealous moments from home.

We wash off hastily made-up white face, tell ourselves we're home.
Starved: how family keeps coming up. Coincident deserts course "home."

VIII

The body continues, despite the dead; how close
We do come, at times, to that slowness. As close

Our bodies oscillate, minutely, always. Such near
Drops into that early deep set us off—disclose—

Foreign growing motions. We three had no idea
What pull might be, what stone; it encloses.

Such spinning still encompasses more than three—
In a warming wound all are doubled; a fist closes.

I remember the body continuing, despite the dead
Close as choked inside. I remember what comes after this.

IX

It takes a certain discipline not to notice, what we chance,
Not to ask, "What are we doing?" Trust a war to enchant . . .

Is this your first breath of gas? The very first hand,
Willfully put to fire? Between us there isn't a chance.

Mine came smothering, to kisses awake, eyes sewn
With dreams of death by orchids. Doubting, gave fire its chance

You'll thank God for someone else to forget, a thing close
For kindling. Awful yes, but against such terror, our best chance.

Breathless, your want falls away; this is our way, blood will out
Snow will go to water, as shame fades. We'll take the chance.

X

I set out to find you with no idea you might be.
My thought of gravity, *yours*. Falling, to figure or, to be

Shear density of absence; below me, the train,
A breaking accident further down time broke, audibly.

The metaphor, running to ground, cracks, the proof of it.
I miss you in your house. Dwell within what's not to be.

Still, on the Viaduct, weighing between fear and a wish.
I could walk away. In fugue, wreathe round what used to be

Our same haunts. Falling, as some boy I once was did. Dead,
Or twinned, becoming rumours crescent now, to Araby.

Who could refuse? The beloved, of indeterminate sex
As a wager. I am, are you? Happily, you needn't be.

Further down the line, you do not hear its heart stop,
The survivor of this body. Not what you could use to be.

What Daphne Wrote Georgia

I

What a heart is, is forever at risk. Reborn to you,
I know this, and to that condition, consent.

In your eyes, disclosed, a singular deprivation:
Your want is turned to passion, it is steeling.

And when we turn to boys, rare with thirst and trust
That our becoming might remain ours

You threaten, giddy and rudely, you promise
To devour me roughly, to take me wholly inside.

Under your mouth and in your hands, I become again,
So protean as to survive that, more, to grow wild and lovely.

Beloved, consider a carefully cultivated flame.
Of how it is that I want, with you.

II

How shall we make our way between Jerusalem, Misra, Beirut?
Before time falls upon time, loose sheaf of translucence.

Do not tell me the day is gone, and the night is gone;
between them, love lies like a kiss, the word's cataclysm.

You avoid promises, warding curses, bad fortune.
Your opacity is an achievement I should marvel at.

Or, emulate. So the future might not notice,
Your touches are that light.

III

I do not know how you came to dwell in this,
A room as low as my heart to the ground.

I do not own this room, or, in your dwelling,
A body with rumored tears, to comfort, to hold.

I do not own this tomb, or, pretend to   You,
Do I ask but your consent to be generous, with time?

How is it this room is filled with bodies? Their skins
full up with sand.   Forget that.

I do not know, if you came to bury here, why—
Could we not leave the past the future, now?

After Mahmoud Darwish's *Beyond Identification*

1.

As in a dream, memory's fall out
of the television, sitdi or jitdi say,
Here comes the haunch man selling you out.

A lover once, asked "where am I now?"
as we all were asked, asked ourselves
we all who have come to live in a city

When the city turns out of itself, exhausted,
        And coerced by its new masters
And uncle says, "Nevermind."
We submit our dreams for review
There are days we can do little else
                Forfeiting memories

In Beirut with his hand on a car door
And then the push of light and force
And then no longer his, nor hand.

When I was turning dangerous and newly made
In a shorter skirt, with dubious associations,
My uncle became cautionary
Significantly, within the words, a journalistic form

2.

As in a dream, in the news
memories fall out of the television.
There is the haunch man selling you out.

A lover once, as we all were,
we all who live in a city

newly turned Beautiful as girls
must ask "where am I?"

When the city turns out of itself, exhausted,
        And coerced by its new masters
An uncle says, "Nevermind."

We submit our dreams for review,
lattice of lace, a war from elsewhere,
From Id to Real ID…
between me and my cousins
Status updates our new breakfast table talk
        forfeiting and counter memories

In Beirut with his hand on a car door
alight with time,
And then no longer his, nor no longer hand.

Nothing waits, it anticipates.
the push of light, across the Meditarranean
across the Atlantic, flying blood
and a cry—
Back to the family home.

Later the anxiety of a plane going up or down
The question, what do you report? For whom?

My uncle become cautionary
Cautions, within his words, a journalist, for whom?

Uncle became an uncle, "my" cautionary, mouthing
his words, but the heroism of the metaphor.

I write poems about a country I have never been.

A journalist does not emerge unscathed.
Why should he? Who goes back to the family home?

Tumbling the pine cone in Diman,
By way of television, explosions of Rafah.

Reading *The Book of Suicides*

I

Sometimes death begs permission to approach
Sometimes we are confused, death and I

As to your desire, I've lost the language
Fire whispers, tongues of black sun.

On this anniversary, of the flood, of mourning
Muddy earth rises, mute cushion to the fall.

A ray of light, your face, runs amuck
It's just, the moon in shards, for shame.

Veiled, pressed to the ground, and proud.
I fell long hours to endure this peace.

II

A change of sex is not a suicide note
Or, it goes across death, to a particular word

Veiled, you lie in the sun, your eyes wet
With what body are you   leaving?

(Turning earth over, a sign, you hope, of dawn.
Sigh for the last words, the night she left behind.)

Suppose, when next we meet you do not know
This face or flesh, suppose my name is changed.

Reincarnated, skipping over death, the lovers.
I know you distrust the tale already.

III

Where who is dead is a different dead
Or word for who is a rose, has arisen.

Where this death is not spoken
Or a name that we stumble over, apologize after

What Rose kissed, you and her friend; the gloom
Hung low and red between young lips and that light.

My book of suicides began with the thought on your brow
With wine, and snow, a country house and poetry.

Neither Ghalib nor the world did imagine—
But they knew three sexes, tangled bodies' heat

Words read in your mouth, on that night
First love, its death, forsaken, your promise.

IV

The third sex is always dead to the first
Transcending, to the second, susceptible.

Where seducing is a virtue of finitude
A rose is kept for your garden.

And wilder growths allow you to imagine
Vast expanse beyond slant pale of headstones

Neither the world nor Ghalib dead, imagine—
Your promise fulfilled, snow rising to heaven.

Roses bloom inward, a minuscule infinity
Bubbles of earth aflame, efflorescent with air.

V

Sometimes the dead are known to wonder
At this pass, or their past, with love

Veiled, in your room they cannot help
But want, what you've wanted, as if you

And they were in love, and your tragedy
Warded their own, gave language where

Before there was only slant pale of moon
Empty dark pierced with empty light.

Sometimes the dead are found wandering
Wordless, and dismembered, failing to recollect.

VI

A change of sex is not a suicide note
What is a crypt? She heard him with his word.

Veiled, crossed out, divide of his mouth still open
She made her up—a language—we can only imagine

For the future, divide of the world still open
Not man or woman then—angelic, childish, feral, undead

Language keeps its secrets, pink tongue roses, blooming
The intoxication of death or you, a body becoming its own

Name or sounding it out, slivers of cool wrists
Broken, inscribed as accident, an accent encrypting

A change of sex, the languish of your shadow.
Or the sounding bell of this word's breach:

What a sex is, is *forever* misled.

Language Becoming a Girl

if i called you "darling" you would know all words are laden
    what's next? you might ask, roses?
   well, i'm in the grip of something you won't like
      & i might call you (& you
               as a prelude to stealing you away
the delusion i could call (that you must answer
                       must be symptomatic
     of what? my rapture in proximity?
         my lack of ego boundaries?

            the other night, we three (i thought we were three
               the perfect revolutionary couple
poised for   radical intervention, engaged art and hot sex
well, my mistake, and thank you (& you
             for your protests
because i was caught up in my own narrative, careening towards your
thighs, your lips & yours,
white tusks shining
        like knights on white chargers off to slay sexism,
you know, though progressive non-possessive, wet and wild,
               truly liberatory
my dispute with penetration
          could hardly be called chivalrous (or disinterested)
     after all after the demo, you're to love me, need me, fuck me,
right?
         & if this poem doesn't do it, nothing will)
nothing will,
   and anyway what's
one more cock
    or less (unless)
   donning these fake names in crimson
        casting seduction as sedition

like Cixous' seamed stockings
            i manage to beg, ask, force— the question?

who is writing *in* the feminine on whose body
            whose cheesy equation of *the feminine*
       with desire
     is giving, getting
             off here
         and *who* slips

this is between you and who and me, just the three of us
            who will trace, task, turn whose bodies for whose pleasure?
          who's dumping whom?
     or equally,
   who says we can't make a home of pain for us all?
        who says,
                  ain't that romantic?

you & you, ever practical:
        we've had enough of mutilation from our enemies, thanks,
           don't really need more from our friends
               why don't you go ironically venerate Madonna
           or masturbate in theory or

   rather be painting a girlfriend's toenails or my bathroom door,
editing a 'zine or myself
   but, yours in struggle,
                 us (you (& you))
but
       wait, wait! does this mean we can't even do genderfuck sometime
                         wax our legs or
                   nostalgic
don birkenstock drag
       with linked arms so earnestly
                handsome
                     march into the future?)

okay who's pushing now—
                    you two take it
you have your love,
                    I'm stuck, stupid in dust motes
                            in the fever of light, in this unfinished poem
lodged in my spine, shivering and wanting you & you
                    to efface myself
            to say
                            the poem wants
                                    to emerge in a body of love
                            to be dispersed

ii.

s/he's wearing her hair the way nostalgia does
mirrors, tucked behind ears
under reversed baseball cap s/he boundlessly
collapses in to you, these touches,
your in)difference
more than s/he could hope for
given the shape s/he left you *in*

            as *in* thirsts, as *in* ghosts, as *in* as it gets
                    (and out of
                    all her—enveloping frictions
                            touches of, the very *inside*)

never has the hystery of this body been so un/clearly
            a case of his story (that old saw)
            going madly after hers
            après hors
                            this *in* seme(s) less
                            in sides taken, turned
                                    out of, or,

                    after
            boundless
                    compared to
you're so big, how can s/he come to   (be?
only this body
hysterical and less,
                    reliable?

                                        in any frame some skin is in
some skin's out
memory snapshots exclusive clubs
membership ascertained
                    at press of skin
the condensation of self

                                        is this *realization of body*
                            an *in*habitation of desire?
            (the *in* s/he needs
                        after breaking up
                        (some wind shield
                                some bloody fist
                                    on concrete)
                    memory of you/her
            confounded obliquely
        embers raw lips
lapsing   these now girl kisses
s/he says:
                    the new girl is no
                            thing to me
                    no girl now not like you no way no how not ever

        maybe it's just:
"the unconscious oedipus complex takes the form of a k/not"
        a can/not
            and you cut it
            said ballsy:
                                cut it out
            leading her to decide s/he could not find you and
        now I'm not too cordial as i cave on your demands

but before
        your words "how
          like a boy,"
                hang there unspoken
unspeak me
like a boy cannot be spoken
          lips close about— uncut my tits, my clit,
                        my womanly body
       unslice through
          us like children hungering
me all wet gushing
pussy mess talk
 what kinda?
          pussy must talk "me"
kiss and teething tongue seething
  childtalk tied
   you toss me
like a boy
              out the window, into the ruins
moving on, to your next sweet
              love
         unkiss me unkill me
why don't you
and how dare
you treat me
like a boy

horsexe/whore sexed
         —hardly a fit subject for desire
             speaking the whole story of a sex (k)not spoken
/hor plaisir/our pleasures were telling
      the (h)our of an other us,
         fragments of three sliced from a crowd
    & piled on top of,
       s/he's possessive still
scrawling out game plans
         on the memory of the back of a napkin
    balled and tossed   in a dustbin:

in order to go awry you must confide in strangers
desire strangers' desires
hide the flicked tongue like pimp
riding silvery sloped in humped backs
gain their trust

you may say "that most repulsive hysteric" but s/he's getting used to that,
anyway, spent a long time rehearsing this little sign play,
           no supplement to your absence, *dear*—
your body gifted elsewhere to a straighter talkin' straighter shootin' boy

i.

                    funny you're not here to hear
               funny to think of more innocent endings:
                                        that night in the bistro
                         the possibility of another route to love
                              opened with your words:
                                        not so like a boy now
how did you read my fidgeting blush
          arms curled one round one round small of back
                                   straightjacket styled and rocking
                         fragile, never more
                         sorry for my part in making
               acceptable that cut of 3,
                                        2,
                                   1

          sorry i cut you
out
     ·up   we all drift,
               now
                         you say
you cannot hitch here
                         your voice is
gone

33

             along these roads
gone
       is what you were   before i left
                        always following her
what i left to be
             i became   i came
                            alone on the road
        s/he's come undone
               with a stranger
     half frozen
to myself
    leaving
        you turned me   *out*
        taught me

you can't hitch in to love
   love is closed like a sign
   saying "Closed"

          my i knocking against it all night long
               wanting *in*

mouthing *all the rights words &*
still
         your can't is loose
             i'm loose in it
    your incantations
        lost
           your love hits hard on the road
        this body
over
   written &
opening
        s/he sees
        why you didn't want her
      as difference re)cedes
    our ground moves,
         her(e horizon

in this reel July is humid
    (an *Ouma Seeks Ouzo* intertext to Laura Killam's *and
    hands, open* & Erin Mouré's *Rolling Motion*)

i am the one who lies   slowly   & closer
to your possible arm
and possibly rain comes (in the window)
intimates
mouths 'open'
enters unspoken places, open(s
a tangle of sheet half conceals
our looking unbreakable
(that is, innocent)
our coming clean,
looking   to be direct
harp fingers pluck furious
(rolling) what we hold here—
the lineaments' possible blur
lips' and shoulders' ease against—
hips fuse
part
re   fuse.
the fans' slow turns hold the room up
(all the air in it, up)
the rain is still in the air
geckos chill
separation of soft bones   *through the entire scene*
i am the one who lies   *in the real*
(this has been established   *we know there are no*
metaphorical, with the rain   *geckos in montréal*
which does not yet fall)
or possibly
it does
through the entire scene
it fills in forms, de-signs
a complicity (the rain is the possible)

35

your words are sweat   with it
because we are lying still
pregnant, even alone
                and my waiting hot and bothered for another 'long gone'
                        must seem a strange and metallic error to be in
                for those who have not yet begun to hear in their shoulders

here in your shoulder it's another story
i know, the rain
doesn't ever stop   *its exit*
being metaphorical
it's a wash of falling down city in steady sodden desolation
its tearing rents in air
it's tongue scarfing sexy down throat to thorax
it's saliva gathering in moon faces open
pearling at the lips
rapt—
in this reel July is humid
& we are, now,
    twice removed.

where skin breaks

where skin breaks
your stockings are white lace from Valenciennes
i hitched through there once
                    and your garter belt too
that was where i first thought
"you can't hitch in to love
love is closed
like a sign, saying 'Closed'"

but you can hitch in to Valenciennes
            into desire or its hook
                        & hitching in stockings
                            can teach a boy things

&
once upon a time i was—
                        how to miss a fist singing for a face
                    ditch a lift to a dead end
            talk dirty about schoolboys
                    suck a driving man's dick
                        cave before tongue, stubbled lips

your man hasn't been to Valenciennes or to his knees,
doesn't notice the intricacy of the stitch,
the pains you take:
rouge smeared into nipples lips cheekbones,
your coffee burnished crimson
or again,
the faltering scents
of jasmine, licorice, rosewater
lingering behind knees
between wetted lips
    & tendrilling round shoulders.
and why should he
thinks he owns you

and people are often careless of their property.
it's like breaking waves on stone
                    this looking for you
          near sleep but not in it

i see you pealing out of
this little black rubber number
fitted like your very skin
you're in his studio, his
hand's on his cock, his
leather pants are open, his
eyes are complacent. you're
teetering on those heels, my
hands miss the arch, your tree branch spine
my eyes are not complacent—
while you dance before him, feel them
lash you, like a scourge

don't know how i got here
                         near sleep but not in it
wandering wild eyed and wide open
for days
                    months
          years
                                   looking for you
     how many years?
tearing through these skins: male, female, female, male
                         until the body's ceased to matter
                              the body never does cease to matter
what finally comes to—
          it's time to take you home
          time to simply take you

my hands are in your hair and i know that you can feel them
your eyes are half lidded but you're nowhere near sleeping
the cock i fuck you with is ridged and lined with pearls
i'm tasting the blood beneath and the salt slick upon your skin

and where my hands have passed you already love the bruises
and where skin breaks open i'm already deep inside

are you burning love?
　　　　　blushing is so slow . . .
　　　just remember whose blood it is
　　　　　spills

through slipknot bound wrists you tie with such easy grace
the kohl smear of my eyes, the blood swell to my lips
the silver rings piercing tits your fingers hook and twist
the cock you make your fist cracking my ass wet and red
and the hot dew of your breath condensing on my neck
and the hot draw of your cunt sticky cross my face

it's like that
　　　　　　the dream i have you
　　　thrashing, just trashing me with kisses
　　　　　　　barbed, with holding still
　　　　　　　　kisses
　　　　　　else blindfolded at my feet

　　it's the back and forth you like
　　it's the break i ask you make

Fawn gets Orchid, or,
either Fawn gets Orchid or i do

Fawn was into leaning into gas lamps that August, her head full of airy filth and hung with nuclear fever, long and silver laced, breathless, she stank of fruit candy kisses, her pussy tingled at you, and meat packing, you put it into language. you were a bear with calloused paws rubbed raw off cobblestones and wrapped them so craftily round her tits she didn't even notice, just fixed her lips pure and studied in the rearview mirror.

you thought she looked familiar.

once out of that heat Fawn was a girl, sure. cool and composed for all the feral animal language wrapped around her lupine supine bovine feline canine ursine lines and signs composed so exactly at the caress of skins no lone stranger friend could tell her for what she was, she was not.

Fawn bared girlskin that night, leopard print hip huggers, and his hooves were cloven, begging eyes and big jugs pointed, navigating the steel pole limo. shimmied round the hot tub faux leather fields forever and your gritty
ingratiating smile. closed in that exposure he felt about him only jagged steel, teeth spring-loaded, couldn't tell if she was having fun. under the leopard print the deer girl the shattered bones the memory lapses the straight A student boy next door in his big sister's underwear.

in those days he was writing poems. in a poem he once was falling from a hand giving love to strangers. he ran into you, Orchid, and that prelude was never published. you happened to be his absolute, not incidentally.

with your hands up her asshole for a million billion years she was foundering without a thing beneath her feet. you brought out the her in him. until you dumped him in the gutter. until she found you again.

Fawn was naughty that night, not nice. she didn't know what to do with you but she thought it should hurt. still she was not so proud as to deny herself

40

the fantasy of having you again. let's just say, in her kissing and killing you oh so swollen and purple, she felt a definite affection. "let it take a long time," she thought. bored her plastered-on dagger nails as black as black as deep into your thighs as they would go. and left innocent for the moment cherry red lips plumped around incisors the size of her cat o' nine tails swishing fondly between her legs.

II

and now Fawn's feeling smeared by you, Orchid (by Orchid's death). you're
difference marked in real and what real is, is the thing she can count on, next to her, Orchid's skin. your skin is cold skin, Orchid. this is annexed and the one is yoked to the dreaming other, as if difference were the first thing before kisses or bruises or as if those were not residing in difference and Fawn's feeling bruised which also darkens with kisses pink to plum and though it's been sexy before it's been real, this time it's different and you are no longer a lover, Orchid. you broke her right off, here at knees and arms, and since ashes ashes all fall down she's determined you will too.

and she's feeling darker because she got you and you deserved it (even if you didn't deserve it) and you're lost to her, here. this becomes the most hurtling fast difference she cannot catch up to, get next to

III

in another universe things worked out differently.
there Fawn also became an assassin, which is also sex training, but she took up dark painting metaphors to soothe herself in her mornings. she edged the names of Dutch masters (Bosch and Bruegel and van Eyck) into margins of countless Persian carpets and felt a little better for the open thanatos in her eros, her little bit of milk and sugar.

and so the night she finds Orchid, and straightens her out (dead), it's not purely a righteous thing. Fawn is envious in all her black leather, watching our scene. repeats memory snapshots like whip cracks on Orchid's thighs and still in her skin, fast welted skin clings to manacles–what kind of crack tastes like her mouth, hungry tastes as if my hand could fit all the way in?

ecstatic (ex— static,) we have no bones limits and skin carries through skin, steaming. she fears this endless is endless

but she's turned on too and in that universe she can go with it. i can't say why it turned out different (in our universe). we should have gone with her to the fine arts museum more often.

it's just we get lost in what's just, shards. Orchid attends me still as you used to, deftly springs into her chains ready for my use—but that is so mechanical you might say to her—what of your difference? your abandonment?

poor puss, weeping for days swinging in the breeze when your faults are not reprimanded and with that she and i converge, old girlfriends admonishing a testy novice.

you're laid out flat on the glass peering through the restaurant skylight where i drip white wine on his tits and butter fresh from the creamery melts at the press of her thighs jiggling and curved as a spoon turning in pussy. idylls—

*

because we dream this later it is fantasy
an imaginary other
dimension
and not real
Orchid is dead in the alley
because we dream *this "later"*
(it is fantasy, not real)

*

Fawn has a hungry mouth here too, taut and thinned and (this is a nexus in this or any dimension) she has a fantasy she doesn't know what to think about: that she is a boy, tough and swaggering, in the navy with her own skinflower, a pretty past now her future, a whore who shackles her self to bed each night hoping for violence
for something to dig   into

something like you, Orchid, only not dead
walking around, a girl about town—
Fawn watches you sometimes

wish fraud

how do you commit that?
you're spinning gold
your needle craft to a name

this is where your hands should be
instead, slim aging hips

perhaps that's unfair, queeny dramatic
how do stars descending
reconcile

i was born too
i live near, by the ocean
used to.

when some one asks you [] to be brave
[used]

a stitch in time, feral,
metonymic, don't get

used, to be born
to ice the wedding cake, you might walk in [] circles
[shrinking]
unsteady, the consequences
as soon as you believe in lines
believe?

and how do you judge my mother
my brothers, sister?

the truth [] my love, I dare you.
[splitting]

you remember
you took the ferry
you walked on

the pond frozen at 4 am
frost in your hair

do you want the thing you are not yet
to love?
to fuck?
to exist?

there is still [] one
[some]
in that question.
there a snow covered lake, there a highway, the full moon
. . . a long way to drive . . .

eventually you [] fade.
[run out of questions]

inland
i don't know where that is
how to orient

an inside drift
what fierce eyes, what sharp tongues
you have

you don't know when you will fall
where the men bleed like women
by the phrases of the moon, marked

after the melt what is,
is given up, there, a stain you can
derive or grieve if you must
i lay thrown in August grasses

if the body,
tears?
tears is a word.

when you come across it
lean, i ask as a favour, lean

notes toward dropping out

This is where I ceased—
Not to be too obvious,
        or in
mutation, or distilled, transmogrification

Beauty queens don't do so well in grad school.
Even if every body wants one
When you assume the shape, austere, assume anything.

            Thing it, sister, thing itself, thing it loud to last your girl
                    Black Lips Cool and Quelled

In the '90s every white body wants a theory for becoming, other.
Don't let D & G fool you, nobody wants one to become other.
        Even if Saturday Night at the Pyramid, BoyBar, ClitClub or
        just hanging out

If you want or do become other, it will be needling
                        you will be false-ly accused, charged with
                    falsified access to a rare and dangerous

        Paramilitary
                designed by I, Desire
grooming rumours and splitting mythoi
like rage and glass, sick with genre
for fun fun fun
not likely.

Nobody wants to become nobody.
 And authentically so, they fear.

What if y = just being
Yours sincerely

Yours truly
Yours until the very end of days
Yourself? Being, as k. would say, "an edge predicament"
?   Beloved, in Kind.

There are two kinds of people in this world,
binary and
non-binary, or
Suppose we did say we were a third then that were a word for
capping it off, or anything more than
                              the tyranny of the couple, or
Momma and Baby and Daddy makes
moon enough and time...

There are two kinds of love in this world
Narcissistic and Anaclitic, or
Ana can't get over how dependent upon
Narcissus she's become lonesome after all these years.

Love to love you, baby, in theory
but   say you do get out of this library, theory, club,
how are you gonna make it North of the Wall again?

There is a cabin in the woods, a secret way,
a drunken ruse   time untravelled   stolen back

So, Mummers and co . . . children, etc. . . . . Arty or Sexy, etc . . .
        Abandoning Incest and Deconstruction no more than your God

                    If you are on the moon, or off the moon?
                    If you are seeking a body or displaying one
                    run off dreaming carny, corny and carnal

Still no body wants to become no body.
Remember that when you are discovered
                        in all your figura
                              borders of the Real, surrounded

    clashing arms and legs
      even sleep is aching with it

while Glory bathes our moon with massacre.

49

Hysteria of Origins

.dora's Machine

[handwritten note: 'Pandora' – reference to 'Pandora's Box'. Hidden secrets – locked away evil?]

what sex was I?
don't ask, don't tell
give it here
keep it safe, a little keepsake
from the good old days

sometimes veering a girl/ flung
aground/ it's nails hanging on
the force of the explosions
the unbounded questioning
(unhinged, you shout—*Make it shut
up!* —slick razor daddy, i loved you so
even with your tools and your big ideas)
a then verging boy with such pretty hands
uncertain stare and auburn curls
scrambling for the key
like for dear life, for the inevitable *afterward*

[handwritten note: Transitioning – neither boy nor girl]

but if harmony can be abrupt—
like a white sand beach
you came with a manual
cribbed lines from Hall, Woolf, Stein
telling me *to decide*
telling me *not to say*
telling me *keep it closed*
and so, I apologize
but again—explosions—

all those ruined telephones
can you help weeping at my voice?
reaching halfway across *The Ancient World*
the tears that come in rushes
and the funny look they all have
at the teleboutique

sizing up the *one who cries*
the destroyer of telephones
the *inevitable* questioned afterwards

what boy virgin opened
a girl verging upon
a question,
the dissolution box: — *Pandoras box*
my cut up boy body, cut into girl body
if it, if that meticulous

can I just say HOW HARSH you are with me
your only baby?
forget it

*Talking to "Daddy"
memories come*

i met someone today
a galore of terror my sweet love's name
won't come on *Hope*
won't come on *Perhaps*
but on a knife's flared edge
a midsummer night
a world become liquid, irradiated.

                                    this body you won't touch

in gathering folds
humbles the ones you love, fierce
over the respirator.
don't tell me, i know already
how things end in different places
how, here, they already have.

*A lot of references in some poems to
Greek mythology —*

53

Tiresias' Confession (. . . in the snow)

white is the colour of the icebox
and the drunkard's confessional
the urinal. a cool, analytic

making up scenes, white is endless
(as in love) as in *what lies under?* this room, too.

Figure *it* on a couch, at the analyst's
I kid myself, think this is *over*
In '97, you are off *farming*
my obsession is   benign
is *love* is a *gift* is *not*
a *mortal sin, not a demand, notanobsession,notadestruction,*
Willnotresultinruin, in
Ruin (we are all to come to, out among the . . .

innumerable future weddings, pictured, in the Sebastopol graveyard)
looking at the ceiling go icy to think of it

tombstone impotent, even before the hormones
and this chemical castration is at least a guarantee against rape—
was that ever a threat? no, I don't think so
though every pill conceals a city full of open windows
premonition
any possible window's
fall, sounds a future found

the things you learn about snakes, eh?
wanting, to be the beloved
wanting, to woo the beloved for the rival
to be the beloved of the rival
to fix the vectors of that triangle
forever, angling obliquely toward survival,
laterally against playing
judge, jury and executioner, for all my sex

which sex? who wins?
not the sex of

imposture: a cool, analytic
pissing distance . . .   from our little comic masque
how like a boy
to take the long view.

Aloysius, stenographer

I will draw you in by breathing
I don't like the way you dress
I am lost to the deep water
She said, go unto the people.

> *My problem with literalization, getting*
> *drunk at Rob's house in the woods means*
> *I must want you. It doesn't help*
> *you strip me bare, give me instructions,*
> *but really it is just the echo of the townships*

Put on a pretty dress and sexy
Breathe into my mouth a murmur
Heart it with your chelo sexy
And purple scrawl along her drawls.

> *To the extent that the triangle*
> *is a repeating animal or you*
> *took me violently or I invented you*
> *(and you) missing you as a result*
> *death is a slow cooker.*

Thighs chalky and chunky and splayed
Tongued ringed and irritated sprouts
Hallmarks of a dragon torpor, Aloysius
In my life I loved them all.

Eurydice's face turning

refusal
of any forward (too forward) putsch
          or revolutionary movement
          it's warm here, after all

and who turned first away? in a glaring thrall of light
an inevitable reversal
becoming, your double, her negation (don't balk
it is not you who is dead
you, who, still loved, beloved by so many
must live and I
having failed to sustain my own resurrection
and gone below the ground   *i*
take my consolation)
this death is less troubled than the last
each death is easier, that's what serial killers
say
(and police) and policing my sleep, rooting out these
slivered mirrors of our intimate rapport, our psychic bond
makes you, my infamous stalker, regress to other bygones
earlier departures, indwelling girls, and each turning back
cuts slant through skins
earlier wounds grow florid and pulpy
          Darling, awake!
my earliest deaths should have prepared you for this,

remember me (no use, but go ahead, try to resurrect me, your indwelling
mirror to song, I—here, you're singing right now,
kissing the lids of my eyes, such round stones harrow
you're kneading wet clay, needing my thighs)
          —it's all so clear to me now:
the way you've displaced me onto all your other loves
Thracian girls dancing with blades and rouged choir boys
cinders of us then and thin   you've grown   sicker and thin
on such milk as ashes give   i give you a few years
i leave you now

             to your hunger, these imaginary dialogues,
yearning for the interruption
you can not anticipate where i would cut in
moving lateral, sidelong hurtling through space
just the same we have traveled just now
to the same place in the ground

was love any different from this
departure?

Orpheus, *the Muses' return*

Sometimes you can say, *This is language
theft,* sometimes, *This is gorgeous blood.*
Sometimes you take the winding path
to the water, sometimes, in to the shore.
Sometimes, when you have been skinned, *snake!*
You kiss the one who peeled you,
slowly and with method
with infinite submission.
Sometimes the bell she has curled
of your dermis
flutters in the breeze,
an inverted tulip   *(nine aflush, prophet!)*
some other you might stumble out of.

I liked nothing about parades
except maybe you
in your tux and tails so handsome
leatherfag girl in straight boy drag
a hot day in the park.
Seeing what was coming
I nearly wept
spoiling the picnic
nearly.

Indiscriminate imaginary seasons of
girl on girl on tongue
I could be the whole town going down on
your cascading thighs
some high school snow white.

You took in what was yours.
I relied on that.
Red mouthed in the quad
one hand clasped, the other smokes,

feigning indifference
as girls do, not hearing
their jealous whispers
lezzie   fag   lezzie

You'd think (we were) making
out on billboards
in trendy punk 'zines.
You'd think all these live gigs
might get you somewhere
might get you out of all this—
inevitable
kiss,
          kiss
fuck it—

I want a formula, like I used to want music
first you put on a dress,
your old red dress
then start shooting men . . .
raise the dead
Don't I wish, but, even still, we are held by Eurydice's last words:

Invited to a party in a backhanded fashion through a mutual acquaintance,
you are told to come unaccompanied, that you must leave your lover behind.

If you go, there are photographers, and you are caught
forever or until the death of film.

If you go the hostess may revenge herself upon your sex,
on your imposture, on her inclusion in this poem.

If you go you leave your lover behind and she may go
to the waterfall and wash you off: blindfolded forever you will not find her.

Neither vision nor song is much comfort.

If your skin is becoming, a bell of desire, words ring out of you, blow
                                                                    away,
truths sure, but you never hit your own; still you kiss the thief of your
tongue, though you miss sometimes the art.

Sappho avers

Phaeon:

I wake
change sex
(yours) and clothes
are piled high, and near our
float of mattresses

the refuse of *metamorphosis*

in your new man's body
you get addicted to collision
your apprehension evanesces

finally, a legitimate target
you'll hold my hand in public
i dance around you barefoot
like your child

(in my journal i mark x for the times we make up
you slap me silly   *brute!*
we make up

dangerous words
like "our . . . mattress"
make you squint your eyes
where once you might have
scribbled them down)

you, the romantic with the spray paint
ready to hitch on/across any old thing,
you want to switch again
and again the hunger for trans-position
makes even imperfect substitutions
preferable to a body at rest

it's an amateur Shakespearean thing
i tell you
there are a finite number of variations
and you won't like the end

following fashion we invest in black leather, pins and needles
faster/slower becoming machines—
animals—
machines—
The black oozes from holes in my tits
You accept that that is scary. Then you're the first to say
maybe we should stop.

We don't stop.

Saying rosary on a bike chain across your back   i
loose myself in hot piss on the floor of the confessional.
Is it that cold in here? It steams as it hits you.

In New York you've become legendary with the club kids.
I worry because you've given up on poetry.
One day you won't come home.

Sappho:

what sex was i?
some girls only play with knives
maybe after? what sex was?
bored monsters, in the queue at the clinic

when I was a crazy boy in New York City
verging no longer across sex
but into the dead into phantasm
all I could do was walk fast like racing
weeks into months without sleep

walking the streets a litany drowning
a girl I was also knew cliffs rich with poppies
ocean's endless breaking upon
and the ventriloquist's trick
and looked for solace in the breasts of young girls
what you call sirens

and so, with your eyes turned elsewhere

who can live in refusal?

brilliant exhumed chests I've come to exhibit and
pray you mistake for art something utterly other
a stupid and mannish thing in danger of being

stretched between holding on and concrete descent
we can say a body has a certain tendency
between one fall and the next

and so it's not personal my refusal to leave this place
I was a beautiful girl once a *young* girl and you
less averse to the smell of cedar
my native isle

who looks for a solution
in bigger girls? they're poetry now
the question: what is in between . . .
Phaeon, such pretty calves you have

one of several threats to this or any
salvation narrative

"you have a nice face"
given one turn of hope
oh, for something as small as that . . .

before I was dead/
when I was a boy, it was ambiguous

between me and burglary
how I approached women:

seduction experiments
and some of them, fearful

going out seeing being seen and the disappearances
—steady, steady— "reality is metonymy"
you ask too much, and tender less than a kiss

an accident we strive after
if we two align on a line on the page
after poetry, genealogy is the melancholic's art

without a present and your body, now
how to explain
verging between girls, boys (over) takes me
out of my too eerie and sad skin
—the beauty of snakes—
worshipped from the Bowery to Lesbos,
abandoned and famished, just the same
don't you
wish you were?

Enduring This Future

Psychic Fair
    for Noel Knockwood

Spring, 1983. You probably won't remember.
You were working a gig on the outskirts of town.

A man, not much older than I am now.
MicMac in the colonial way of spelling. Reading
Auras. Spelling calling casting. Sagebrush from California,
or—something, scented your tent . . . I think you wore plaid, braids.

I think you had his name, but as a teenager with issues
who wasn't and isn't a . . . ?
            I didn't see very far
beyond my large and, I know now, attractive nose.

I'm not sure how you knew.
I mean, I "know" about Two-Spirits, thirds, and fourths,
I've read the anthropologists, and know some folks now
who've talked to the grandmothers, ones who can say....
but Mi'kmaq man, the church was forced on your folk for a long time
now.

But what you saw, what you said.
It fixed me, still, and I was thrown, known.

Okay, well,
it could have been the smudge, of my eyeliner,
it could have been my pointy toed boots. Was I wearing a skirt?
How could you have known? No one else did or said, or not

before you and your medicine. It doesn't matter.

Your gift was a curse of freeing, dread and hope
of what I already knew.

You saw my— medicine?
And for years the way I would tell the tale,
mangling my thanks, it's some settler gothic thing, even now:
I met this old Indian man, and he told me—
Telling, he made me, with a word, a story, this girl.

Fata Morgana (Ferial Mirage)

She awoke to an appetite for narrative. Wanted to know who was a memory machine. Who was a memory. She was in a bed and she was entwined and twinned with, and she was nearly thought (the moon) she was nearing the moon. Two in a bed and the Witch, was it? Under the moon, heavy breasted and plunged into it. It was only scary. What recursive thought isn't? She awoke to the moon, full and flaccid, stinking of drunken sex, sweet with it, like a child.

The romance is always two in bed and in another room, another. Some fey thing you thought you cast off, full. Under the moon, your familiar, you're twinned with her, twined and strung out. Halfway across the city, or, its architecture. Your restlessness at six a.m., an appetite for water or memory, the sweat of it. You have the feeling of a wolf. Feral idylls, ferrous. The taste of sickness in your mouth. A moony child, switched in the night.

Two in a bed and through the window a gray line where dawn will come. It allows silhouette: trees, clouds, horizon. Her eyes on her lover rapt, knotted in Celtic shadow: silhouette. Whom she wakened to, in her appetite. The feeling of a wolf or a child behind the door you locked. Or, the eagles wrapped around my neck, at the collarbone, martial. Love with its histories of war and open to the band of light, at the horizon, the willingness of light, its capacity to diffuse, to allow others, palest blue, a yellow awning of dawn.

A witch, sucking her tit, beautiful as her familiar, and the precise articulation, the immediacy of tree branch silhouetted, black veins with an upward reach. Love against the dawn, sienna dissolving slate. Here with the bones of the trees we're still in night, but the mist's uneven line speaks of how day may come through trees; they're horizon. It's a winter night anxious for day. Two in a bed are debating with dreams, which to allow. Which to wake to? Children under foot, whitening. Too long with a pillow over her head.

Smothering is something you can't argue with bones. The past is the past and children should not get under foot, in the pretty jaws of a witch. Outside the sky is plunging trees. Clouds enjoy her sleeping smile. She is mindful of snow on the tracks, widening distance, a capacity for depth. With colours coming as inevitably as old lovers do, or not, when you are in danger, or asleep, out another window, the city skyline feeling its own: blue thinning of dark. Your love is walking the rounds. The chill air is working its way everywhere like smoke into sky. Where diffused, every dawning is refused. Like memory, like children. It is a matter made from radiance. Your concern for freedom.

Where her freedom was concerned, the witch had her aversion to trains, or trials, of thought that might ask of her—a certain lightness. She got out of bed, distracted with her moon and an appetite for water. Memory flooded the dawn with others. Dawns she had cast off, not unkindly, but with an instinct for survival, and now? It was all comparative and her love enjoyed her sleeping smile. Her teeth hurt.

The city was lightening in the west and still she felt refusal from the moon. Full, and indifferent, the cut of her thumb from dinner the night before. Acid with having you, and unable to sleep. She was to be pulled a cloud's distance. (Once there, we would be with others.) She was aware of the necessity of certain fictions, more certainly of their failing. Often, she flattered herself, she was above all that. There were gulls in the widening distance and as a lover, as someone with some measure of dignity, of freedom. What gulls at early dawn, pulled, as she woke to snow, a little hung over, and dishes to be washed. Never the less she prized her freedom. Stole yours. Love demands that, and one needs to be able to work. A certain distance, and *then,* or *until,* the backward swoop. Fiction will do that for you. More, if you are a beautiful girl, as she was, and determined to be.

I swept over you before I came downstairs, and said sorry, not for leaving but for the before. My restlessness in bed and your sleep winched to the moon, which was being insistent with me. A fey child, locked outside and scratching, leaving a certain sickness in my mouth. One tries to be fair.

Last night, putting on my beautiful girl face, and playing with my hair, you are sweet to me. I need some water. I meant to say: she woke with blood on the narrative. The taste of it, ferrous in her mouth, and the feeding of the dawn on night, nearby. How do you sleep through that? Luminous and plundering sleep, whole breaks of colour, ask the impassibility of light. Where gold comes through palest, crimson tendrils, mauve surrounds, and palest, gold comes through. The sky and last night's party, all that red wine, leave their furrows. It was only the nightmare of the last time that kept us in fiction. A certain distance. Overcome. For one of us, or one moment, anyhow. The sun came up. Time to wash.

She awoke to an amber flush, gaudily more so. Deeper ocher, deeper maroon. The winds were at her and what they carried. Silhouette intruding with a sharpened edge, and her perception pierced with it.

Surgical Diary

Oct. 15, 2000

This is A's hand writing, not mine: *(not quite)*

For reduction of bruising, swelling and muscle/tissue soreness:
arnica homeopathic encapsulates undertongue, you will want daily
may vary your intake while you heal
will help you notice
you'll heal daily
arnica tincture as liquid applied directly to your skin on sores

For reduction of scarring:
lavender essential oil after tissue is closed, you are closed, not weeping in
your skin vitamin e is also effective, after you're tissue healing, it goes in
closing
after it is

Icepacks feel terrible applied directly to you to your skin go
directly on swollen tissue where you are bruised
immediately after surgery for three to four days
directly applied will significantly reduce swelling

A humidifier might be useful
you'll have a hard time breathing
you'll heal dry

(A's curls fall in the finely knotted leather of a flail, the red of blood welts,
remembering
her voice is crackling sugar, where normally as smooth as warm maple.
More than most A's face both composes and
conceals the designs of beauty.
Today, she is generous with a history she suffered.)

73

Oct. 16, 2000

I had my last consult today. Three surgeries in two hours. I can't believe it.
I'm not sure what we agreed.

I said: *I don't want you to make my nose too small.*
He laughed.
I said: *I don't want to look like a white girl. My nose is an Arab nose.*
He said: *It's unusual, but . . .*
but you want to be pretty? To look like a woman.
I said: *Yeah, but I can be Arab and be pretty? A woman? My sister has the*
same nose.
There was a pause.

He smiled.
Many Arab women enjoy having a smaller, more delicate nose.

* * *

Yael's got everyone's email. They're making a schedule for the first week at
least, and then we'll see. I'm going to be well taken care of. I tell myself I do
need this. I won't be able to make my own food, maybe I won't be able to
stand up. How do you know yourself in the midst of such loving care?

Oct. 23, 2000

I think we're going to go on strike. I wonder if it will all be done by the time
I'm walking again. Among our more controversial demands: medical leave
for transitioning transsexuals, financial assistance for sex reassignment
surgeries.

Millot writes that we transsexuals make a demand upon the Real, for its
adjustment. Just so.

Oct. 26, 2000

The question is how I can here try to rewrite this body which is less truth than occasion, which is making a bargain not with a fantasy but with fantasy, all the distortion that entails.

That's a lie, the second to last thing. The fantasy is specific, singular. (Having been a serious marxist boy, and a good feminist, I may have a hard time living it down. Or out.)

Oct. 29, 2000

Tomorrow, incisions. And something fuller. 375ccs of saline in a silicone shell. If my skin will stretch that far. Apparently there are instruments that can tell. Submuscular, so my tits won't ripple like a pond and pebble collision. The incisions (tomorrow) under my arms, how much of a stretch, to get them all the way in? I'm hoping my nipples won't point outward, we'll see. I expect my breasts will be bigger than I expect because everything is imaginary and ideal right now.

I couldn't make the party last night. My friends are so loving, there are no words for it—
They're curious inevitably. But it would have been too much to see that many people so soon before. I kind of felt I should though, given them a last look at the pre-surgery body. There's something seductive and strange about imagining my body as public property. Why?

It's just going out to party, being part of *the scene*, you know . . .

(I say that particularly in the habit of antiphony. And hard now not to feel (your) absence as anything other than conspicuous. A space of whiteness very near the centre, I might be very nearly staining what is seen (obscene).

I have these flashes, I have to confess, where none of this is my doing, where it is all me being done to, at the behest of someone unknowable and undeniable. It's a story you've come across before.)

75

Nov. 1, 2000

Going in and under was easy, science fiction, because for years I used to lie in bed and imagine my surgery and it was the future. It was early in the morning we when we left.

There was a waiver to sign. I felt calm changing into the paper gown. The nurse took some photos, and I walked into the theatre, which felt very small. I lay down and my arms were restrained, so I wouldn't shake the drip. The drip knocked me out, better than those old ether masks. Passing out was from childhood too. I don't know how many times I went under as a kid. It's always their talking while you fade that is most warm and scary.
I don't remember the trip home.

Nov. 2, 2000

When he drew the packing out of my nose, I was afraid the blood would get everywhere. He said my lips were already healing and that I needed to come back in a week for him to check my nose and my breasts. He decided to make my breasts larger. He said they looked too small and that he knew I wouldn't want that. I made a show of being outraged.

We had trouble getting my meds. The pharmacist said she couldn't fill the prescription because the name on it was different from what was on my insurance. Yael took care and explained everything. The pharmacist understood perfectly. She refused to call the clinic to confirm Yael's story. Yael was near to tears, she was so furious. At the next pharmacy Yael pretended she was me and paid for the meds out of pocket.

Inside, my chest tears and pulls the lengths of my arms. Every motion has a measure of pain, that is almost calculated (somewhere else) in the time between motion and sensation. The mind is more quickly trained by this severe and immediate flesh than I am.

I cannot believe he wanted me to do this without codeine.

Yael's catching some sleep on the couch now, while I sip my soup.

76

Nov. 3, 2000

Gender Dysphoria (dysphasia)

I used to think dysphoria meant falling,
to fall out of, or even, within,
Not unbearable and so I used to be
Falling out of   not just
Bearing with the difficulty of mine
Of being a place and its erasure.

Nov. 5, 2000

Mostly today, I am floating, bodiless, and I am an eleven year old at
Christmas or home sick. It's time for ice cream and soup. Though soon . . .
Odd that reading children's fantasy now would evoke such old consolations
and escape routes, just days after the surgeries which should have answered
that longing once and for all. As if—

I can walk to the couch on my own now, and it doesn't hurt much so long as
I am careful. It's not as if every upper body gesture doesn't rip at or through
something inside, but there are other muscles. Still all my metaphors have
closed in on my body, and the world is contracted to the smaller square of
this basement. I like the amber of the walls. I really dread ever having to go
outside again.

My breasts seem strangely high, distortions of chest, rather than resembling
. . . It's normal, I'm told, but it makes me nervous. I cannot lift my arms
high enough to see where the skin is sutured, under the arms and
disappearing inward. But I itch inside and out.

Yael is holding me together. My brother and sister-in-law should be by soon,
with their newborn.

Nov. 7, 2000

scared girl
she would sleep next to me, here,
me, anxious of every touch
there is no word for *hers*
she put her skin, there, on the outside

i keep thinking this is forever
like when you're to be married.

Nov. 9, 2000

Questions for the Doctor:

              how to tell healing yellow from?
              what are acceptable fluid emissions?
              how soft or firm should they be?

        (is it strange to ask? what do I know of breasts?)

              when do I get unstitched, or will they melt?
              I can't feel my lips or nose, for how long?
              how long before sex?

Nov. 13, 2000

Woke up with dreams still pulling, and so the day is hazy, not quite in
focus. Could be the meds. Could be the lack of light. Dreamt the scene in
Passion of the New Eve, where Eve meets Tristessa, discloses what
we've maybe known all along, that Tristessa, paragon of cinematic
femininity, is transsexual, or at least Angela Carter's imagining thereof.
Funny to be returning to this book, the one that opened for me the
thought of surgery, having just been operated.

The inscription on the book, *from Dana* is *to Patrick*; so loving, and from

when I so needed that, the world had ended mostly and I was gone. I
remember one day though, Dana and I were in a café in Little
Italy—maybe on Clinton Street—scribbling poems to one another. Like
this entry the poems were nostalgic, sentimental. Nonetheless, they
allowed the future.

Nov. 17, 2000

It will be six months before my body settles into shape.
How many hours of knit before this is not a body and its change?

Don't be deceived.
No, I've not, not yet. I'm not, not there. Or there, or—
Though I can feel something move as if across a great distance.

I keep catching at a length of a rope descending, the slip
Returns your questions.
I think they are your questions.

If desire is always a ruse, why this time or shape?
Why this cut, here?

red like a femme

I

getting the red   stuffed
in like the inbox
when you say femme i hear sex change

        getting me read
we're so eager to
defer her

when you write femme it comes out
incest

figure it out, coming out
and cheerleader movies
have this in common

polish clumps to my nails
            psychic, round like boys, the objects gather

II

I'm sitting pretty

        drawing the red out
her terror,
            wandering
            straight as these stockings

you know,
transsexual femmes always wear our stockings out.

you know?
how important it is, we keep them straight.

III

I'm finally in, folding
          for her name
why femme feels like
childhood, what becomes your voice
is what she hears, spirits
taking that name, i learn
your knowing

anasemia
kisses close
after the red
     the reading

IV

popular variants on the scenario:

i dreamt myself butch like a mac truck
in heels and glitter stumbling into you
how should i say your name?
     a straining   falls away in   your voice from California
     bared, or when you enter the room in a new dress by prada all eyes turn,
                                        you're just
sayin'
          "my name is a holy name"

in that song you sing   we let loose femme's lesbian context
instead select
saline filled silicone
          with a black fringe, purse
          tucked
from the diaphragm rising to end each sentence
leaves a bright red smear
about a something cock

red as for grievance, black for eulogies overdue, if she is seen to be
transsexual, a girl to die for, really
be relieved it's not her for a change
missing
          in your body.
don't you hold with
                 what got said? i'd
halter a long vowel
rather than travel still in those closed circles
                      and yes, sigh, lesbian
and be grateful for the graze of an unknown hand.

June 15th   a fragment

I

blindingly bright
waking you do not now know
even in this—
anguished beginning of fear and determination
this year of things breaking

where, in what conflagration or bruised
body posed, opposing
transecting the force of a structure,
you think, the word for it once was fascism,
when opposition composed still
the ground composing speech
      or allowing
what makes sense,
so far from where you will be in a few hours, at 3 pm

waking you do not now know
in what breaking weight descending
call the baton for what it is, an intent to break you
      apart, to partition a body or a movement
to make the pain particular
      encompassing, exhaustively, yours

you will need to dig hard, to work to recognize
in yourself in such a moment

in the reach or range of love or rage or
in the torrent of a common frailty or
in the push came to shove of inarguable necessity
the capacity to, if not overcome, then endure
your fear, and holding it
move forward
make it to the end of the day

II   Carleton @ Jarvis

wanting to write this day,
this churning within the city,
at first all i can think of is you asking,
half joking, if it is possible to conceive a
People's Militia that is not a swift
descent into petty fascism?
I'm thinking we can have this conversation because the day feels nearly
over. we're lingering, falling nearer the back of the march,
feeling safer away from Queen's Park, past 52,
you're goofing, swaggering, butch;
I'm so gonna kiss you.
i see B go by, blinking, the pepper spray mostly gone from his eyes,
K is buying water, L is in the hospital concussed—
we don't know that yet.
glancing over your shoulder, you see
the hard line of riot,
the geared up cops,
closer now than you thought

III

joining the march midway, having slept in
having drunk too much the night before
talking about whether or not to make the march

at first it feels the same, like a hundred other demos,
the first major one of the spring, it feels like spring,
it feels like the right thing to do, it feels like cruising, it feels safe.

I've hooked up with some queer girls, anxious
they may be friends of my ex—
I'm surprised to see gas masks. I've been away, things have shifted
while i was

IV

i am watching my lover at the demo
hanging back, keeping as safe
as her stomach will allow
moving forward, in fear for her best friend, C
who is dancing
skirting in and out of the front lines.
these lines are moving, broken but moving,
C seems fearless, today

I am watching R, confronting the cops,
who are screaming orders at her or
trying reasonably
                    like nice reasonable cops
to get her to back
away from the slight rise where a statue
has her back and join the others,
other protesters, just a few metres away
where the less reasonable cops are beating them with plastic shields,
with truncheons,
trying to rout them, with horses.

i am watching the horses, eight or twelve,
for some reason i cannot count, i try, repeatedly but *i cannot count*
their riders are pushing them to full gallop and we
are resistant, scattering; they're pushing, riving   through

my love and i are on one side, with perhaps twenty, perhaps forty others,
somehow those eight or twelve riders on those eight or twelve horses
are driving us pushing us, out toward the road, into traffic.

stumbling backwards, careful not to run
i am watching someone fall to her knees to avoid the swing of a baton,
i am wondering what force that might possess,
coming from a man on a horse moving at such speed.

i am watching the horses go past.
my love says, "We should join the others.
We should be over there."

V

even in traffic
crossing a road
should not be so difficult
with so many bodies
here though
we must also contend
with so many ways of being run down.

VI

we leave the gardens
for the hospital.

in the gardens i do not see
the armored mass swarm
faster than you'd think.

no one does get to think,
about that; the media has already gone
to report the decisive tug and break
of fear, into action
under the header
"Violence at Queen's Park"

so that when my brother watches the news
and says to me that he cannot abide
"the violence" he is not speaking
of the provocation of the state,

the brute force of the cops,
or the forty plus reported deaths by exposure on the streets.

he is not speaking
speaking, he is,
        not knowing
brilliantly blind,
        his own violence
the polite complicity
  of the determinedly neutral and prosperous
     who bring us in to this time
        where we are, all of us, called
to face and force
     this uncertain work of making in breaking.

Ballard's Angel

Lying on the warm concrete of the gunnery aisle, he assumed the postures of the fragmented body of the film actress, mimetizing his past dreams and anxieties in the dune-like fragments of her body.

J G BALLARD, *The Atrocity Exhibition*

Ballard's Angel has an articulated hard-on, it never goes soft on—a gleaming chrome stick shift to drive between the legs, Ballard's Angel lacks—black wings upgraded with customized chopper blades of accordioned Damascus sword steel twirling like Ballard's Angel's propeller shaft issues out the backless silver lame frock clings to Ballard's Angel's curves like a spoon turning

Ballard's Angel has the same measurements as Jacqueline Kennedy, who has the same measurements as Marilyn Monroe (tacky Jackie O, oh so coy beneath that blonde wig) who has the same measurements as the 1962 Lincoln convertible her husband virtually died in

Ballard's Angel morphs, like on MTV, like *in*human mercury, like shattered glass melted and blown out again, like high speed digital imaging you can do at home, like the god Proteus transfixed at the mirror, speed freaking

Ballard's Angel is like Athena born from her author's skull bursting from internal combustion

Ballard's Angel is a faceless pink female nude jetting blood from bullet holes in breasts so pert she casts the shadow of an American Stealth bomber, was it the U2 shot down by the Russians in 1960? She is mindless and writes autopornography with her body, she is orphaned in a dun coloured landscape
that makes absolutely no attempt at realism, bombs drop around her, she is virile, dead, she aches just like a woman, but she is not, a woman

Land Day (March 30, 1976)

The government said "Security and settlement" and called curfew
for Sakhnin, Arraba, Deir Henna, Tamra, Tu'ran, Kabul
sent in 4000 police and the IDF . . .

Ysrael Koenig advised they "cement long term Jewish national interests"
and "examine the possibility of diluting existing Arab population concentra-
tions."

Without land,
       and your fear, you are not you
                    robbed of your face, spirit
and in no place to lie down, how
        to turn, rise,
             fly upon the moment?
  We all want to be light
        Know light's plummet
        Lose ground.

                  This is to come to land.

If a child is a land you may not own,
If this child is called Impossible morning
If our histories make us lie,
If down
If, in *home*, blood soaked

                        If

    Too many trampled and trampling feet
      too many laws bulldozers soldiers laws bulldozers
crowd where your house,
your olive, fig or lemon trees should grow.

How might you live, if you do not take back the land?
You may not own, but for land, they mass.
              It is a word stolen.

Furious

The Greeks gave vengeance disposition.   Snaked hair kin,
Gorgon winged, fearful husks from aging women into
implacable law, clawing after punishment.

> *Our beauty whispers*
> *the most intimate of betrayals*
> *murder of a parent, rape of a sibling.*

That pleasure might purchase
three inclines to darkness:
prelight or eclipse, a long journey into hollow.

> *In Rome we were Furies, from Furore, madness.*

Scholars always blame the hungry dead. The usual root:
something stolen somewhere, underground, a stumbled upon
crime—a struggle, you with the land and this, my heart-hollow
made up bombs, lingered in the curve, round echo of old longing.

As if me, you dreamt: someone should call the furies.
Or one already has.

Time itself is confused by the particulars.
What's hate in such a state that stands to slaughter
those whose dwellings it raised, those created
in its own image: looking glass survivors, looking glass camps.

Without a tongue or some inside I couldn't help but
mangle this self, your speech, pangs of ether, other
birthwrack of testimony.   Suppose that were a promise?

> *Where you are, we were, and will be again.*

Call that a threat or terrorism, something sick, made up
in a laboratory clinic. Am I here, or there, any less likely to betray
entranced by the seeming--
        seamless consistency
            could we call it beauty—
                        of a particular species of hate?

                    Do you see us, everywhere, hamming unsubtly,
                        in love with our own white bones?
                            Holy hate, full of basking,
                        a lover's face hovering in a window
                    slyly pleased to be in the observing, observed?

                    Is it too much, to boast of how we make a dwelling,
                        in a desert, a shelter for battered women,
                            a summer camp, for lesbians?

So limber, just in from limbo, this hate comes
versatile as a child, exuberantly becoming
larvae made hate's cocoon,
butterfly, hate takes wing.

This hate bears children with names like amnesia,
nothing to me, nothing to do with me,
and butcher's knife.
Who is not to love the offspring of such good neighborly hate?

                    Rich reserve of those especially near, intimates of your breast,
                        those whom, joyously, you turn away, we bury,
                    with all the compassion left after the glee of amputation.

Do you yourself know this hate,
find yourself in its attachment to separation,
Partition?
We have all done its work. In a small way, I do it now.

It is thick and drawn around the necks of our common inheritance, or enemy, debts of love, and shared oppression.

If not for such pristine hate, keening cleft
 might we not become such entangling beings,
so closely confused, anarchaic,
more expansive than friends, lovers, or children, more open . . .

> *Lover, we keep hate precious as secrets,*
> *a blade closer to hand than sister, lover.*

It has proven curative, quick and progressive
As with, for example: expelling the queens
from the Pride Parade,
inviting the transsexuals off of women's land,
casting the whores from Cabbagetown into the lake,
driving the Palestinians into the sea,
just as you feared, you were warned,
those others intended to send you.

Is it possible now, even to ask, who will hold off the bulldozers,
who will cook beans and rice, who shall shear the skins of those
grazed with a daily glance?

Can we manage without these gun handling hands,
The help of your genetic code?

> *And don't you yourself hunger for whiteness*
> *falling over your shadow, hate*
> *that male body, that oppressor's dick?*

> *Becoming a girl so fair as if snow is, does it not show, everything falls?*

How to withstand a hate that disposes of bodies
without questions, as though it owns them,
the way we own the bodies of our sisters,
brothers, parents, lovers?

Shrouds sewn of one cloth
no outsider would dare step in
even stop by, to inquire.

With hate we are adept at severing some you from we until they fall
away—

> . *we were cut loose ourselves, many days we are cut at still, are we not*
> *entitled to the use of our own knife?*

All frenzy beneath the silence, our fury
enjoy the elegant demonstration of   *our* rationale:

> *only one shall survive, if any, and*
> *your chances are so much better*
> *if only you embrace our logic of sacrifice.*

Ghazals for Sharon Cohen (Dana International)

I

In the defiles—a Jew, or, assembling the signs
Of a detour. Landing, her parents in the camps.

Neither sexed nor given to Arabic in the home.
Can you believe it? In Israel? Of Israel?

In Palestine, we know, four hundred villages
Ceased.   For that, "In the beginning . . ."

Do you dream of Yemen, Dana?
(As I dream of Lebanon?)

In Europe they praise you, *Diva*—
Jews have not always fared so well.

II

Sharon is singing, between two languages, three.
In your second sex, improvised mother tongue.

They say you corrupt the youth of Cairo.
That you collaborate with *Mossad*.

At home, *Likud* and *Shas* denounce you.
"Home" is burnt sand, disappearance in light.

Later, your songs are banned in Germany.
They say, Arabs and Turks are the new Jews.

In a feminine voice, what hazard's presence.
In your house, is there shelter, in Palestine?

III

"The Girl for 2000," beautiful, transsexual—
Web banners we all aspire to

Embody. Emboldened, the possible this night
Glamour, for ever freedom's caprice.

As in air or errant, as in love, I imagine
Cascading translations' incandescence.

What a body wouldn't do, shall, in time,
Transpire, breaking lines, a people's musculature.

What comes before? Cherish your singing voice, Sharon
This moment of dwelling toward the sky.

Draughts of Purim

one day to the future, an uncountable past.
harbinger,
who doesn't know, why

she is, what she brings. Y,
you cannot approach
your enemy open,
not, knowing.

did you notice, i was
pursed slip of silk in the dark
her gone white and back? you

didn't know to whom I was,
i didn't—
wanton turn to
that brace of friends, her
enemies, to know whom to love?

an army of course,
ruinfull, of such clever girls
not to speak,
but sign

when it changed
Y, she, I,
we got it in the face

did you imagine migrations
escape from triangles?
a special dispensation to travel
Sfat, Basra, Beirut?

even come a changeling
you're no more intransitive
than sex, for instance

was that before or
after that night?
or after unrecognizably
after imperfect

      what a girl was—
witch stain, swollen wind
kissed hair
always ask, before asking

not to impinge but
a dagger to lips you marry
silver turning marrow and muscle and silk
all ablatives restless   it
looks like it's morning

why masque the terror you fly to?

Afterword

The conditions of possibility for making art, poems, criticism, as an "out" transsexual, transgender or genderqueer person have expanded substantially since *Wanting in Arabic* was first published. So too have the incentives for signifying under that sign, which introduces new problems as well as possibilities.

The earliest poem in this collection, "Ballard's Angel," was not only written pre-transition, but against transition. Up against it, and trying to keep the door shut. There are versions of (lesbian) feminist thought and left critique that in vanguardist fashion would prefer some positions stay subaltern, remain spoken for and "merely figural." Once upon a time my own apprehensions about transition took recourse in such discourses. Though I wouldn't go so far as to call that "false consciousness," it certainly was defensive. Trying to keep the door shut.

Other early poems in the collection were written in the flux of beginning something that felt unknowable, if necessary, in the rupture that comes of making oneself by breaking through one's self. They carry some of the ambivalence of internalized transphobia, as well as indexing the moment's enthusiasm of a queer theoretical vocabulary (a lesbian post-structuralism) that looked like it might allow trans subjects to speak. That was true for some and not uncomplicated, I think, for any of us; "being allowed to speak."

When Lianne Moyes invited me to submit "when there are three" to the bilingual journal of feminist theory and experimental poetics, *Tessera*, she initiated a process at that journal, one that recognized trans subjects as subjects-in-process, and as subjects of feminism, of writing-in-the-feminine. Which perhaps begs the question of Écriture au Trans-masculine. That's not my question, a question for my poetics, but it is a question that suggests possible thresholds and aporias between feminist and trans discourses on and of becoming.

Performing my poetry at Mirha-Soleil Ross's *Counting Past: Perfor-mance-Film-Video-Spoken Word with Transsexual Nerve!* in 1997, 1998, 1999 and 2001 changed the mode of address. For the first time they were spoken/written to transsexual and transgender people, performed among and with other transsexual and transgender people— trans writers and artists, community members, friends and lovers. Our differences from one another, from ourselves, were made manifest in ways that were joyous and fecund, as well as uncomfortable and abrasive. Those were good problems to (finally) have. The promise of the current decade's anthologies and symposiums cen-tering trans poetries and literatures was, for me, prefigured in that festival, though again there are crucial differences in politics, location, locution. The poems that have been added to this edition have their origins in rudiments that were not ready for the first edition, but which marked out fissures in how histories and discourses interleaved to make my own writing possible.

While trans identities, subjectivities, communities and their relation to writing is an axis for this book, it is only one of several—Lisa Robertson's in-troduction gorgeously teases out, elaborates, another, or perhaps several un-der the sign of another. In fact the poems in this book draw upon diverse and contradictory poetic traditions, and one could ask what holds them together if not identity? That is, if they are understood to be held, to be together.

Tim Trace Peterson suggests that interrogation of "rhetorical form" leads to a question of what to do "after you've introduced yourself"? It is a good question, one kari edwards might have posed, noticing as it does that while stories about identity are necessary, they are not adequate to the demands of politics, poetry or desire. Perhaps what these poems are then is a series of attempts at inscribing something, or better *some things*, between the nec-essary and the sufficient: things like an erotics, like a poetics, like a politics. Reading my own poems now, later, I see them as attempts to liken or refer such things to embodied and collective subjectivities with both "a contrapun-tal air" and curiosity about what's next.

Trish Salah,
Winnipeg 2013

Acknowledgements

Versions of some of these poems originally appeared in *All Things New, Arachne, Borderlines, Descant, Existere, Feminist Studies, Fireweed, Hence, The Moosehead Anthology, Pawn to Infinity, The Peak, Queen Street Quarterly, Tessera, Willy Boy*, and in the collections *Bent on Writing, Brazen Femme, The Diasporic Imagination* and *Ribsauce: Montreal Women's Performance*. "Land Day (March 30, 1976)" first appears in *If a child is a land you may not own*, a broadside from Flat Singles Press. In the years since the publication of the first edition, many people have reviewed, re/published, taught and written about these poems, as well as supported the work with readings. Deep gratitude to the editors, publishers, critics, teachers and curators for their support. Most especially, because she has done all of the above, often and brilliantly, thanks to Margaret Christakos.

Many and varied thanks are due to those whose friendship, support, critique, love, and inspiration enabled these poems to be written and to see print in the first place: Gamal Abdel-Shehid, Joan Anderson, Sam Anderson, Ronda Arab, Dima Ayoub, Dana Baitz, Rima Banerji, Elena Basile, Katherine Bateman, Dana Bath, Dionne Brand, Andy Brown, Chloë Brushwood-Rose, Gwen Burrows, Anna Camilleri, Brad Colbourne, Julia Creet, Faizal Dean, Jennifer Duncan, Corey Frost, Glenn Gear, Dina Georgis, Anju Gogia, Adeena Karasick, Ailsa Kay, Ummni Khan, Cat Kidd, Laura Killam, Nathalie Kouri-Towe, Constance MacIntosh, Shauna Lancit-Baitz, Robert Majzels, Aiyyana Maracle, Mary di Michele, Erin Mouré, Brian Noble, Rita Paqvalen, Kathryn Payne, Leila Pourtavaf, Michelle Power, Elizabeth Ruth, Sina Queyras, David Reid, Kaspar Saxena, Gail Scott, Gerry Shikatani, Luba Szkambara, Mariko Tamaki, Sharon Thesen, Tamara Vukov, Rinaldo Walcott, Zoe Whittall, Pamela Wilson, Tara-Michelle Ziniuk, Rachel Zolf, as well as members of the Advanced Poetry Workshop (Concordia University, 1992-1993), CUPE 3903, the hence collectives, OCAP, Ouma Seeks Ouzo, and the Stern Writing Mistresses. Deep gratitude to Beau Molnar for boundless support and love during the preparation of this new edition.

Mirha-Soleil Ross, Xanthra Mackay and Viviane Namaste were hard at work in the early 1990s creating cultural space in which a book of poetry by a transsexual writer was imaginable; for that and for their generous friendships, I remain very grateful. Max Wolf Valerio was the first published transsexual poet I ever met, and the late kari edwards was both generous and inspiring in correspondence. There have come to be more names than I could name here, but Julian Talamantez Brolaski, Nathalie Stephens (Nathanaël), and Trace Peterson have been especially good friends in the emerging, exciting throng of "us."

I want to give thanks to my publisher Nurjehan Aziz for supporting the book's first coming out, and for her enthusiasm for the new edition, and also to my designer, Christa Seeley, for her care with the details of this edition. Heartfelt appreciation to Lisa Robertson for her beautiful introductory essay, and to Roo Borson whose critical eye and boundless encouragement helped this book to be, and to be better.

Finally, I want to thank my sister Renee, my brothers Peter and Paul, and my mother Elaine, for their love and sustenance though many changes.

Works Cited

Abraham, Nicolas and Maria Torok. *The Wolfman's Magic Word: A Cry tonomy.* Foreword. Jacques Derrida. Trans. Nicholas Rand. Minneapolis: University of Minnesota Press, 1986.

Alcalay, Ammiel. *After Jews and Arabs: Remaking Levantine Culture.* Mi neapolis: University of Minnesota Press, 1992.

Agha, Shahid Ali. *Ravishing Disunities: Real Ghazals in English.* Hanover: Wesleyan University Press, 2000.

Ballard, JG. *The Atrocity Exhibition.* New York: Re/search Books, 1990.

Brossard, Nicole. *Mauve Desert.* Trans. Susanne de Lotbinière-Harwood. T ronto: Coach House Press, 1990.

Carson, Ann. *Eros the Bittersweet.* Champaign: Dalkey Archive Press, 1988.

Carter, Angela. *Passion of the New Eve.* London: Bloomsbury Classics, 1983.

Cixous, Hélène. *The Book of Promethea.* Trans. Betsy Wing. Lincoln and London: University of Nebraska Press, 1991.

—. "The Laugh of the Medusa," in *New French Feminisms.* Ed. Isabelle de Courtivron and Elaine Marks, Trans. Keith and Paula Cohen. Cambridge: University of Massachusetts Press, 1981.

Darwish, Mahmoud. *A River Dies of Thirst.* Trans: Catherine Cobham. Brooklyn: Archipelago, 2009.

Fanon, Frantz. *Black Skin, White Masks.* Trans: Charles Lam Markmann. New York: Grove Press, 1967.

Freud, Sigmund. "On Narcissism" and "Mourning and Melancholia" in *The Freud Reader.* Ed. Peter Gay. New York: Norton and Co., 1995.

International, Dana. *Diva – The Hits,* IMP Dance, 1998.

Irigaray, Luce. "This Sex Which is Not One," and "When the Goods Get Together," in *New French Feminisms.* Ed. Isabelle de Courtivron and Elaine Marks, Trans. Claudia Reeder. Cambridge: University of Massachusetts Press, 1981.

Jabès, Edmond. *Little Book of Unsuspected Subversion.* Trans. Rosemarie Waldrop. Stanford: Stanford University Press, 1988.

Kroetsch, Robert. *Completed Field Notes*. Toronto: McLelland and Stewart, 1989.

Lacan, Jacques. *Feminine Sexuality*. Ed. Juliet Mitchell and Jacqueline Rose, Trans. Jacqueline Rose. New York: Norton Books, 1982.

—. *The Seminar of Jacques Lacan, Book III: The Psychoses*. Ed. Jacques Alain Miller, Trans. Alan Sheridan. New York: Norton, 1993.

—. *The Seminar of Jacques Lacan, Book VII: The Ethics of Psychoanalysis*. Ed. Jacques-Alain Miller, Trans. Dennis Porter. New York: Norton, 1997.

Millot, Catherine. *Horsexe: Essay on Transsexuality*. Trans. Kenneth Hylton. New York: Autonomedia, 1990.

Mouré, Erin. *Furious*. Toronto: House of Anansi, 1988.

Rushdie, Salman. *Shame*. New York: Knopf, 1983.

Tolbert, TC and Tim Trace Peterson, eds. *Troubling the Line: Trans and Ge derqueer Poetry and Poetics*. Callicoon and New York: Nightboat Books, 2013

Willis, Danielle. *Dogs in Lingerie*. Zeitgeist Press, 1990.

Wittig, Monique. *The Lesbian Body*. Trans. Peter Owen. Boston: Beacon Press, 1975.

—. *Les Guérillères*. Trans. David Le Vay. New York: Viking Editions, 1971.

Woolf, Virginia. *Orlando*. London: Penguin, 1993.